T0158808

The Gift of INFERTILITY

For God's gifts and His call are irrevocable.
Romans 11:29

Nnenna Okoro

WESTBOW
PRESS®
A DIVISION OF THOMAS NELSON
& ZONDERVAN

This book is a work of non-fiction. Unless otherwise noted, the author and the publisher make no explicit guarantees as to the accuracy of the information contained in this book and in some cases, names of people and places have been altered to protect their privacy.

Scripture taken from the HOLY BIBLE, NEW INTERNATIONAL VERSION®, Copyright © 1973, 1978, 1984 by International Bible Society. Used by permission of Zondervan. All rights reserved.

Scripture quotations are from THE HOLY BIBLE, NEW INTERNATIONAL VERSION®, NIV® Copyright © 1973, 1978, 1984, 2011 by Biblica, Inc.® Used by permission. All rights reserved worldwide.

The Scripture quotation noted NKJV is from the NEW KING JAMES VERSION of the Bible.

The Scripture quotation noted KJV is from the KING JAMES VERSION of the Bible.

WestBow Press books may be ordered through booksellers or by contacting:

WestBow Press
A Division of Thomas Nelson & Zondervan
1663 Liberty Drive
Bloomington, IN 47403
www.westbowpress.com
1 (866) 928-1240

Because of the dynamic nature of the Internet, any web addresses or links contained in this book may have changed since publication and may no longer be valid. The views expressed in this work are solely those of the author and do not necessarily reflect the views of the publisher, and the publisher hereby disclaims any responsibility for them.

Any people depicted in stock imagery provided by Thinkstock are models, and such images are being used for illustrative purposes only. Certain stock imagery © Thinkstock.

ISBN: 978-1-5127-4956-4 (sc)
ISBN: 978-1-5127-4958-8 (hc)
ISBN: 978-1-5127-4957-1 (e)

Library of Congress Control Number: 2016911552

Print information available on the last page.

WestBow Press rev. date: 8/11/2016

I would like to learn just one thing from you: Did you receive the Spirit by observing the law, or believing what you heard? (Galatians 3:2)

To
Abba Father
Dear Jesus Christ
Sweet Holy Spirit

I will make you very fruitful; I will make nations of you, and kings will come from you. (Genesis 17:6)

SOURCES OF INSPIRATION

My journey has been inspired by seven verses in the Bible.

Chosen by God: Genesis 21:6

"Sarah said, 'God has brought me laughter, and everyone who hears about this will laugh with me.'"

Revealed by God: Matthew 6:33

"But seek first his kingdom and his righteousness, and all these things will be given to you as well."

Given by God: Isaiah 35:7

"The burning sand will become a pool, the thirsty ground bubbling springs. In the haunts where jackals once lay, grass and reeds and papyrus will grow."

Taught by God: Acts 1:8

"But you will receive power when the Holy Spirit comes on you; and you will be my witnesses … to the ends of the earth."

Spoken by God: Philippians 1:6

"Being confident of this, that he who began a good work in you will carry it on to completion until the day of Christ Jesus."

Destined by God: Psalm 34:19 (KJV)

"Many are the afflictions of the righteous: but the LORD delivereth him out of them all."

Anointed by God: Zechariah 4:6

"Not by might nor by power, but by my Spirit, says the Lord Almighty."

CONTENTS

"Command and teach these things" (1 Timothy 4:11).

PREFACE

I have revealed you (God the Father) to those whom you
gave me and they have obeyed your word. (John 17:6)

The Life Application Study Bible NIV (New International Version) in
Genesis 1:2 states, "Now the earth was formless and empty, darkness
was over the surface of the deep, and the Spirit of God was hovering
over the waters." The earth was in a state of infertility until Almighty God,
the Creator of heaven and earth, spoke the word and began to recreate the
world. Creating man in His image on the sixth day revealed the existence
of an eternal gift to humanity, a gift that most of the prophets spoke about
in the Old Testament and John the Baptist was born into as a divine
assignment to herald and identify to humanity. A gift referred to in John 1
as "the Word." John 5:24 says "I tell you the truth, whoever hears my word
and believes Him who sent me has eternal life and will not be condemned;
he has crossed over from death to life."

He was precious and beloved yet God ignored His plea during His
agony and tears at Gethsemane to "take this cup away from me." This gift
(Galatians 5:15–16) blessed the world yet went through untold suffering,
crucified on the cross, and resurrected on the third day to establish power
and authority over all creation. It was impossible for His mission to fail
because the souls of all depended on His suffering, death, and resurrection.
Humanity waited from the time of creation, but He arrived on the earth
through the womb of a virgin and submitted patiently as a carpenter's
son until it was time for His ministry to be revealed as the Son of God,
demonstrating power, supernatural miracles, signs, and wonders with
evidence of our gift of infertility.

A gift always bears fruit but also has the capability and capacity to recreate another gift. Jesus Christ sent the Holy Spirit to help you operate in your divine assignment, step into your destiny, and receive your gift of infertility.

INTRODUCTION

Every good and perfect gift is from above, coming down from the Father of the heavenly lights, who does not change like shifting shadows. (James 2:17)

God's purpose is larger than our pain. This book is not about fruitfulness but the gift of infertility. It is about the gift that manifests or is revealed as a result of your personal trials, tribulations, and experiences. The essence of your struggle. The reason behind your seasons and cycles of issues, problems, and challenges. The diamond in the dirt. The ultimate product of a refining process. This gift could be a divine destiny, assignment, or task waiting to be activated in you through the process you are going through and the experiences you are having. In some cases, it could be the following:

- Birth of a baby: a chosen one
- Design of a new product: a trailblazer or best seller
- Start of a career path, business, or ministry: expansion
- Healing of your body and soul: restoration
- Start of a personal mission: new beginning
- National assignment: leadership opportunity

The most important outcome of any gift should be the blessing to humanity, glory to God, and achieving the intention for which it was created in the beginning (Isaiah 46:10–11).

It is our responsibility to nurture the experience required to achieve a God-given vision, fulfill our divine destiny, and bless a generation.

Although my experience in seeking the fruit of the womb and finding fulfillment in my calling triggered this gift you now have in your hands, infertility could manifest and affect other areas of life, such as your career, family, ministry, nation, marriage, business, health, and/or peace of mind. The feeling of pain, loss, confusion, helplessness, isolation, and lack is the same. The end of an anticipated dream that is short of your expectations or a below-average performance is a sign of infertility. Your infertility journey might start from a particular location but could take you through various stages, seasons, relocations, and divine connections before its manifestation. Yielding yourself to the Holy Spirit is key to receiving your gift.

A major consequence of infertility of any kind is the tendency to paralyze other aspects of your life, isolating you. Inadequacy of any kind draws attention to the object or limitation and saps energy from other areas of your existence. For instance, severe or life-threatening illness can cause immobility, which can rob you of your career, business, relationships, hobbies, and peace of mind. Infertility of the womb causes misery and loneliness and denies you moments of joy with your spouse, family, and friends. Infertility of your labor and investment attacks your self-esteem and peace of mind and can destroy valuable relationships. Oftentimes, these experiences are inevitable even for believers; therefore, we must focus on being victorious over all circumstances and trusting Almighty God, the only One who reassures us that He will never leave us or forsake us. Our ultimate priority should be to fulfill our destiny, leave a legacy, and achieve eternal life.

Gifts birth other gifts, but it is dangerous to assume that evidence of blessings placed in your life today is a confirmation that you are working and walking in your divine assignment. Don't find out when you get to the top that you've either been climbing the wrong ladder or living someone else's dream. This book will make you sensitive to uncommon events in your life critical to accessing your gift of infertility. We will explore three core gifts from God and various areas of infertility in other people's lives in the Bible and how God blessed them. This will also appeal to anyone who has felt at least early signs of a new beginning after a series of heartaches, spiritual blindness, unexplained disappointments, and untold failures in life. We will review your countenance while waiting, how your gift is nurtured, and the appropriate response to the outcome. Once again, be conscious of the fact that the gift can manifest before the promise. You are now invited to explore the journey on the road to receiving your gift of infertility.

CHAPTER 1

Predestined for a Divine Mandate

I make known the end from the beginning, from ancient
times, what is still to come. I say: My purpose will stand,
and I will do all that I please. From the east I summon a
bird of prey; from a far-off land, *a man to fulfill my purpose.*
What I have said, that will I bring about; what I have
planned, that will I do. (Isaiah 46:10–11, emphasis added)

"Before you were formed I KNEW YOU" (Jeremiah 1:5). The essence
of forming and sending you through the process of conception was
already issued as a divine mandate. God, the author and finisher
of your faith, predestined you to come into this world and accomplish a
task for Him and humanity. All of what you are, what you do or not do,
what you own or are currently deprived of, what you represent or wish to
become, and where you belong are predestined to navigate your divine
purpose for being formed, made, and born into this world. Think through
your life and seek to find out the essence of your existence. Oftentimes, we
do not ask these questions until life circumstances create infertility in an
area of life that forces us to reexamine our priorities, seek God, and resolve
to find answers. The tragedy, however, is that some people seek this solution
apart from the One who predestined their existence. The womb was part
of the process of bringing you into this world, but the divine purpose for
your life can only be found by seeking God Almighty, Creator of heaven
and earth.

A divine gift is given by God to humanity and delivered through a called and chosen vessel (man, woman, or child) willing and able to go through the growth and maturity process required to execute a divine plan and impact generations. Divine gifts obey Genesis 1:28, where God commanded men and women to be fruitful, multiply, subdue, and take dominion. This divine mandate starts with being *fruitful*. Fruitfulness refers to all areas of our lives. Being fruitful in your body, soul, and spirit requires the capacity to grow, create, produce, innovate, and expand. Fruit of the body refers to fruit of the womb, well-being, health, labor, and investments of time, energy, and attention. Fruit of the soul refers to fruits of the mind and heart (usually expressed by thoughts and speech). Fruit of the spirit refers to fruits of our character and habits. All these should ultimately *multiply* to impact humanity, change lives, and win lost souls to the kingdom of God. Your fruitfulness should be sufficient enough to *replenish* the earth and trigger the gifts in other people. In the process, you *subdue* all limitations and obstacles, taking *dominion* over everything and all powers.

God said in Genesis 1, "Let us make man in our own image," and He reminded us in Psalm 148:5, "He commanded and they were created." Where have you been seeking a solution to the infertility in your career, body, marriage, ministry, or other areas of your life? Where have you been digging for answers to your problems? How lost are you right now in your body, soul, or spirit? How far have you gone in seeking the gift deposited in you, the gift masked by situations you are facing right now? Whose manual are you reading and studying to access answers to life's challenges? The One who made you sent you to earth with a complete manual on how to live, exist, and achieve your divine mandate. That manual is called the Holy Bible. Do you own a Bible? How well do you know the Holy Bible? What is your relationship with your Maker? Who directs your path? Are you really working/walking to achieve your divine destiny and manifest your gift? Whose are you?

Before you proceed to the next chapter, reexamine your life and attempt to answer these questions. Isaiah 46:26 says, "Review the past for me, let us argue the matter together; state the case for your innocence." Whatever you need, whatever you desire, whatever you seek, whatever you have lost, God is able to give, provide, and restore. Stop struggling and turn to your Maker. Turn to the One who thought about a task, selected you, formed you, and sent you forth to the earth. You might be living the life that the world envies, but is that what you were sent to this world to accomplish? "Why spend money on what is not bread, and your labor on what does not satisfy?" (Isaiah 55:2).

If you are living your destiny, impacting humanity, giving God all the glory, and sure of eternal life, rest assured that it is a privilege reserved for all but enjoyed by only a few. This book may not be for you, but I would be delighted to celebrate a co-laborer in Christ and urge you to share this truth with people around you so we can all strive to attain eternal life at the end of our sojourn in this life. If you do not know Jesus Christ, you must stop at this point and surrender your life to God. Confess and repent of all your sins. Ask God to come into your heart to live and be your personal Lord and Savior. Tell Him that you want to know Him more, ask Him to wash you in His precious blood that was shed on the cross for your sins, and invite the Holy Spirit to take over your life. Next, you must buy a Holy Bible if you do not have one and join a Bible-believing church where the presence of the Holy Spirit is evident and real. Study your Bible every day, and never miss your quiet time with God in daily prayer. If you need help with how to study the Bible or to pray, ensure that you seek help immediately. The danger in receiving the Word at this stage is the experience described in the parable of the sower in the book of Matthew. The enemy can steal the joy of your salvation that you have just received before you know it. So act now!

Now that you have activated the thought process and have registered yourself by accepting Jesus Christ as Lord and personal Savior, let us look at the journey to your divine assignment and explore the lives of God's children who went through this process of identifying, establishing, and receiving their gifts of infertility.

Study this book from the beginning, and share it with loved ones who need to be reminded that God is watching over them, ready to perform His word in their lives. Nothing can stop Him.

CHAPTER 2

Created for a Divine Assignment

But you, O Israel, my servant, Jacob, whom I have chosen,
you descendants of Abraham my friend, I took you from
the ends of the earth, from its farthest corners I called you.
I said, 'You are my servant'; I have chosen you and have
not rejected you. (Isaiah 41:8-9)

All of us are precious before God despite how important some people appear to the world. The difference lies in your diligence in seeking out your divine task and earning a place in the kingdom of God. It is not a hierarchy similar to the organizational structure in earthly organizations but rather access to the deep and secret things that belong to God. You deepen your relationship and knowledge of God, and then He draws you close into an inner circle that gives you access to the secret things of God. It's a divine promotion, an honor worth striving for with rewards beyond anything an ungodly life offers. Note that in our text from Isaiah 41:8–9 above, Jacob was chosen even while he was far from his walk with God. He still had issues to deal with until he had divine encounters with God in the book of Genesis. This established his place in the kingdom and resulted in his name change to Israel, reflecting his new standing with God, just like his grandparents' names were changed from Abram to Abraham and Sarai to Sarah when they came into their promise. Saul was also changed to Paul after he had an encounter with Jesus Christ and became an instrument to be used by God. Changing your name may depend on a deeper revelation, but until you step into that zone where you have access to the secret things of God, you may never fully walk into your divine destiny.

Path to Promotion

> Nothing in all creation is hidden from God's sight. Everything is uncovered and laid bare before the eyes of him to whom we must give account. (Hebrews 4:13)

To illustrate this access, I will use names and labels that demonstrate how deeply you access the kingdom of God as you diligently seek your Creator, who loves you dearly and awaits the earnest manifestation of the righteous.

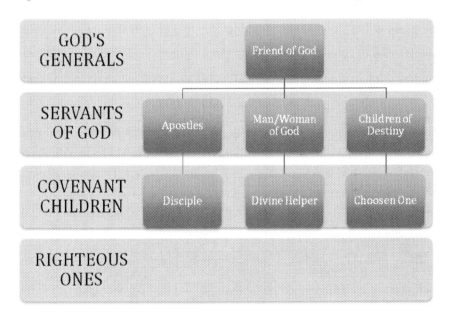

Friend of God

> You are *my friends* if you do *what I command.* I no longer call you servants, because a servant does not know his master's business. Instead I have called you friends, for everything that I learned from my Father I have *made*

known to you. You did not choose me, but *I chose you* and appointed you to *go and bear fruit—fruit that will last*. Then the Father will give you *whatever you ask in my name*. This is my command: Love each other. (John 15:14–17, emphasis added)

These are people who God Himself refers to as His friends. The secret to getting there is *to obey and to love*. Our Lord Jesus Christ clarified this in our opening text. Abraham was the only one God the Father called "friend" in the Old Testament. Being a friend of God brings you to a place where God hides nothing from you. He talks to you directly about everything and sets you on a path to impact generations (Genesis 18:17–19). Jesus Christ made known to His disciples everything His Father told Him in the New Testament.

When you get to this stage, God Himself becomes your shield and great reward (Genesis 15:1). Remembrance and mention of your name produces results and delivers destinies. In 2 Chronicles 20, in a time of distress, Jehoshaphat stood before the people praying and reminded God in verse 7 of "Abraham His friend.'" God responded in verse 15, saying, "For the battle is not yours, but God's." When God wanted to destroy Sodom and Gomorrah in Genesis 18, two distinct activities showed God's faithfulness to His friendship with Abraham. The first one was that He gave Abraham several opportunities to appeal for the deliverance of a nation, but their sin was beyond redemption. The second was the separation of Abraham's loved ones (Lot's family) from the destruction destined for a condemned people.

Only your faithfulness to God will stretch this level out of you. You are able to hear God, become a voice for the people, and receive redemption for your family no matter where they have been scattered physically and spiritually. Generations leverage your relationship with God in prayer (Isaiah 51:2), and God acknowledges a people because of His friendship with you, just like with Abraham (Isaiah 41:8; James 2:23; 2 Chronicles 20:7). What an honor! Hearing from God is important at this level to enable you to execute God's instructions. Jesus Christ described His true family in Luke 8:21, saying, "My mother and my brothers are those who hear God's word and put it into practice." While preaching in Luke 11,

Jesus corrected a woman who hailed His parentage by saying, "Blessed rather are those who hear the word of God and obey it" (v. 28).

Servants of God

> But you, O Israel, my servant, Jacob, whom I have chosen,
> you descendants of Abraham my friend, I took you from
> the ends of the earth, from the farthest corners I called
> you. I said, *"You are my servant"*, *I have chosen you* and
> have not rejected you. (Isaiah 41:8–9, emphasis added)

Apostles are appointed by the will of God to lead, provide mentorship in the body of Christ, and execute a divine assignment. They usually go through immense trials and tribulations to test their capability and capacity for the task ahead. They endure periods of infertility in several areas of their lives and suffer greater afflictions than the people they have been chosen to lead. This is to ensure their sensitivity to humanity. When they encounter challenges in their earthly ministry, God always steps in to ensure that He alone takes glory for their divine assignments. Their suffering often ends with a divine visitation from God either through dreams or visions. Paul's encounter with Jesus Christ at Damascus positioned him for his turbulent but divine ministry. Colossians 1:1 describes him as "Paul, an apostle of Christ Jesus by the will of God." Peter was the closest disciple to Jesus and was present at all significant events of Christ's ministry, including when the Holy Spirit descended on the disciples in the upper room. He preached the first gospel that saw Gentiles receive the Holy Spirit, which triggered Christianity in many nations. In 2 Peter:1, Peter is called "a servant and apostle of Jesus Christ."

Other categories of servants of God include Men/Women of God and Children of Destiny.

Men and Women of God have a divine connection with God the Father, God the Son, and God the Holy Spirit that is evident in their ministry. These are people who have been designated by God to lead a people into their destiny. They have unusual unction to do exploits for God. In some cases, they actually have actual conversations that trigger their divine assignments. Moses had regular discussions with God about the destiny of the children of Israel and how to lead them out of Egypt and through the wilderness until Joshua was promoted to this position when Moses died. The same pattern of conversation continued and Joshua took them to the Promised Land. Joseph was taken from the pit to the palace because of the divine assignment as prime minister in Egypt who would provide for the children of Israel throughout a seven-year famine in the land. Elijah was the prophet chosen to carry the divine message that destroyed the prophets of Baal. David was chosen and anointed as king of Israel to replace Saul. He fought many battles in order to attain his divine task of creating a heritage for the coming of the Messiah. Solomon built a house for God and gave the ark of the covenant a befitting place. These servants of God were privy to divine events or encounters. Moses and Elijah were present at the transfiguration of our Lord Jesus Christ, a sign of their divine position in the kingdom and a demonstration of how God promotes to this exalted position. Spiritual ordination is usually witnessed by anointed ones. Elisha was promoted to function as prophet when he received a double portion of Elijah's anointing when his master was taken up to heaven in a chariot. Another subcategory here also includes prophets chosen to carry messages to a person or a people like other prophets in the Bible and anointed ministers of today.

Do not touch my anointed ones; do my prophet no harm. (1 Chronicles 16:22)

Children of Destiny are people called and chosen for a specific task to advance the purpose of God either by birth or divine selection. Mary the mother of Jesus was chosen as a vessel to deliver God's only beloved Son, Jesus Christ, into His earthly ministry. John the Baptist prepared the way for the coming of the Messiah and also witnessed the presence of the Holy Trinity at the baptism of Jesus Christ, qualifying him for this position in the kingdom. Although the tasks of these children of destiny may or may not have involved positions of leadership, their participation was the key to success for that particular divine assignment, and they received their gifts of infertility. Isaac and Jacob were children of destiny by birth as offspring of Abraham.

A child of destiny may have a background that seems odd to qualify him or her to be used by God. Esther was an orphan, but her beauty and decorum earned her a place in the king's palace, which ultimately helped in saving a nation from being wiped out. Rahab was a harlot, but the location of her apartment and her willingness to assist the spies earned her a place in the genealogy of Jesus Christ. Ruth was a widow without hope yet was determined to find her destiny by remaining faithful to her mother-in-law, Naomi, who encouraged her to remarry and accept Boaz. Her union with Boaz has been likened to the coming together of the Jews and Gentiles, a reflection of the ministry of Jesus. She also took her position in the genealogy of Jesus Christ. Nehemiah was a cupbearer in exile when God chose him to rebuild Jerusalem. Joseph, Mary's husband, received divine instructions on how to help Mary and protect the baby Jesus, a task that divinely positioned him in the lineage of Christ.

Children of destiny are also persons chosen specially to demonstrate God's glory and faithfulness. These include Job, Mordecai, Lazarus, Hannah, and persons who received miracles, like blind Bartimaeus, the woman at the well, and the woman with the issue of blood. Some people with unique and special skills or gifting may fall into this category, such as anointed gospel music ministers, singers, and songwriters.

Covenant Children

> Behold, I have refined thee, but not with silver; I have chosen thee in the furnace of affliction. (Isaiah 48:10)

These are divine helpers, disciples, and other anointed children of God in waiting, chosen for divine assignments. It's also training ground for ministry and a pool for promotion into servants of God. Some of the people mentioned above, such as Joshua and Elisha, were in this category before they entered into their divine assignments. Kingdom children, usually individual contributors, support pastoral assignments, have social influence, or are professionals in many disciplines. They often have a calling and have been identified for a specific task required to support a man, woman, or people of God. The professionals amongst them are assigned to communities or specific projects that will define a generation. They remain influential in supporting a larger vision. It is an exalted position that gives one access to the things of God without the trials and burden of actual leadership. Some people in this category are fast-tracked to higher positions or mentored through a process necessary to prepare them for greater assignments.

In the Bible, most of the disciples fell into this category for their roles in the ministry of Jesus Christ and became apostles and martyrs. Aaron's support of Moses ultimately earned him the position of chief priest. Baruch, Jeremiah's scribe, received a promise of eternal life for his divine assignment. The chief servant that Abraham sent to find a wife for his son Isaac was not named in the book of Genesis, yet his role facilitated the birth of two nations that produced the people of Israel (Jacob's descendants), God's chosen people. Timothy, who assisted Paul throughout his earthly ministry, was often referred to as "son" or "brother." In 1 Timothy 2, Paul called him "my true son in the faith."

It is a highly sensitive position in the hierarchy because these covenant children are vulnerable to trials and victories of power. They are also subjected to the same battles as their masters in their body, soul, or spirit. Some are misunderstood, rejected, killed, martyred, or afflicted. True sons and daughters feel the burden of their spiritual parents. It is also easy for them to become greedy, ambitious, and rebellious. Gehazi lost his spiritual inheritance because of greed. They suppress their innate ambition to support the vision of another but are ultimately rewarded for it. These include genuine Christians serving in different ministries and departments in Bible-believing and Holy Spirit-filled churches across the world. For mature Christians and people desiring to be used by God, it could be the stepping-stone on the path of promotion and into their divine assignment.

Righteous Ones

> His divine power has given us everything we need for life
> and godliness through our knowledge of him who called
> us by his own glory and goodness. (2 Peter 1:3)

You signed up in this category when you accepted the Lord as your Savior. Prior to this, you were formed, created, called, and, hopefully, chosen for a divine assignment. To gain further access within the hierarchy depends on your desire and intensity for a life in Christ, giving yourself freely to God, forsaking all ungodly things and activities. God is merciful, and it is possible for Him to use anyone to achieve a purpose on earth. But remember, doing your task will not gain you access to heaven. Only believing in the One who died for you will.

One characteristic of this category is there is a high level of dropouts. Most people start well after they've had an encounter with God and been given a glimpse of their divine assignment, but they either fail/fall or become the architects of their misfortune. Out of this pool, Servants of God and other Children of Destiny are chosen. These anointed ones are special because they have potential waiting to manifest. They go through battles and periods of dryness in their journey toward discovering their purpose. The enemy would work overtime at this point to stop them from seeing who they are in Christ. They are also vulnerable to the enemy's deception, pleasures of this world, and personal weaknesses.

There are examples in the Bible where chosen ones were derailed and God departed from them or picked another vessel to continue their assignment. This happened to King Saul, and no amount of intercession from the prophet Samuel could restore Saul to his honorable position with God. Cain by birth should have been a chosen vessel, but God departed from him after he killed his brother, Abel, and arose a new generation through Shem. In some cases, a derailed one will bear the consequences but still fulfill his or her purpose. Samson was betrayed, captured, and held as a prisoner but ultimately achieved his purpose even though it happened under undesirable circumstances after spending most of his life in isolation, physical blindness, and hard labor. Others are destined for destruction. Judas Iscariot was a disciple yet destined for condemnation. It was an assignment that was confirmed in John 17:12 where Jesus Christ described him as "the one doomed to destruction." Eventually, it was Judas who kissed Jesus Christ to enable the soldiers identify and arrest him (Luke 22:48).

These examples also show that one could still fall at any level of the hierarchy if he or she does not hold steadfast to his or her divine purpose and trust in God.

CHAPTER 3

The Growth Path

But now, this is what the LORD says—he who created you,
O Jacob, he who formed you, O Israel: "Fear not, for I
have redeemed you; I have summoned you by name; you
are mine." (Isaiah 43:1)

God created heaven and earth through His word, and all the promises
and consequences for living are contained in the Holy Bible. All
throughout the Bible, from the book of Genesis to Revelation, our
Lord God constantly reiterated the process of our formation and existence
on earth. For the purpose of illustration, I use a cycle to demonstrate this
divine formation of you, the called and chosen one.

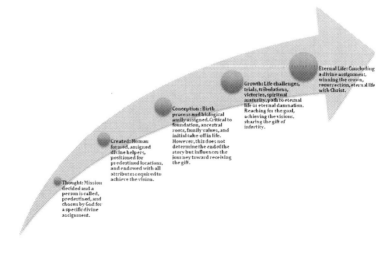

Eternal Life: Concluding
a divine assignment,
winning the crown,
resurrection, eternal life
with Christ.

Growth: Life challenges,
trials, tribulations,
victories, spiritual
maturity, path to eternal
life or eternal damnation.
Reaching for the goal,
achieving the vision,
sharing the gift of
infertity.

Conception: Birth
process and biological
family assigned. Critical to
foundation, ancestral
roots, family values, and
initial take-off in life.
However, this does not
determine the end of the
story but influences the
journey toward receiving
the gift.

Created: Human
formed, assigned
divine helpers,
positioned for
predestined locations,
and endowed with all
attributes required to
achieve the vision.

Thought: Mission
decided and a
person is called,
predestined, and
chosen by God for
a specific divine
assignment.

The growth path to achieving your divine assignment can be steep and shrouded in misery and difficulties. The Bible tells us "Many are the afflictions of the righteous but the Lord delivers them out of them all." (Psalm 34:19). Not everyone will be Abraham, Joseph, Moses, Joshua, Rahab, Ruth, Esther, or David, but your diligence in completing your own divine task will earn you God's favor, generational blessings, eternal life, and resurrection with Christ just like them. God rewards! He delights in giving you all He has promised you. The important thing is to tow your own path, focus on your divine purpose, and win your crown at the end of the successful execution of your divine assignment.

While most people today focus on the glamour of being chosen, it is also worthy of note that the penalty for sin and rebellion can be severe. The expectations of a chosen one can be so high that a single act of unfaithfulness can threaten or terminate your divine assignment or deny you of your gift of infertility. Miriam was struck with leprosy when she led a rebellion against Moses. Samson lost both eyes soon after he revealed the secret of his strength to a woman. David lost a child as a result of adultery. Saul's act of disobedience cost him the throne and ultimately lost everything, including his life. Ananias and his wife died for lying in the presence of God's anointing. Moses and Aaron were denied access to the Promised Land. In Deuteronomy 32:51, God said, "This is because both of you broke faith with me in the presence of the Israelites at the waters of Meribah Kadesh in the Desert of Zin and because you did not uphold my holiness among the Israelites."

"Many are called but few are chosen" (Matthew 20:16 KJV). You have a responsibility in determining how you achieve your divine assignment on earth. It all depends on your ability to love, seek God, obey His commandments, forsake all, and be willing to depend on God for all things. "Seek ye first the kingdom of God and his righteousness and all these other things shall be added unto you" (Matthew 6:33). It is not a life of misery or boredom; rather, it is a fulfilled life devoid of all things that do not please God but completely committed and surrendered to the Holy Spirit. "God is a Spirit and they that worship him must worship Him in Spirit and in truth" (John 4:24). Any deception in the way you work or walk with God will only hurt you and your future, destiny, and descendants. He desires a life of holiness and righteousness from us because He is a holy God (Luke 1:75). These basic rules must be obeyed in order to be in right standing with God, which puts you on the path to receiving divine instruction and guidance for your growth and maturity and ultimately to receiving your gift that will attract generational blessings beyond your immediate family.

Generational Blessings

When your days are over and you go to be with your fathers, I will raise up your offspring to succeed you, one of your own sons, and I will establish his kingdom. (1 Chronicles 17:11)

This was David's gift of infertility for his humility and faithfulness in embracing his divine assignment from a tender age. Despite all his innate weaknesses and indiscretions, God said David was a man after His own heart (Acts 13:22). God declined his plea to build a house for the Lord but promised David that his own son's throne would be established forever. In the same text, God said, "I will be his father, and he will be my son. I will never take my love away from him, as I took it away from your predecessor" (v. 13). So you see that God is faithful and true to His word concerning the chosen and their entire generation. Seek Him, and access your divine assignment required to advance the kingdom of heaven and bless your lineage. A similar promise was made to Abraham in Genesis, and it came to pass when Isaac gave birth to Jacob. Isaac also experienced infertility of the womb, and God blessed his wife Rebekah with twin boys, Esau and Jacob. Jacob became the father of twelve sons that made up the twelve tribes of Israel, God's own people. Throughout the generation of Abraham, blessings were pronounced upon these sons. If you remain faithful, even the very blessing out of your lips to your children will trigger generational blessings and favor upon them. It all starts with one man or woman, you, who decides to seek God earnestly and obey His commandments.

Three things are critical to receiving your gift of infertility and achieving your divine assignment: decision point, divine connections, and birthing process or location. These will be discussed in more detail in subsequent chapters.

CHAPTER 4

Decision Point

Noah did everything just as God commanded him. The Lord then said to Noah, "Go into the ark, you and your whole family, because I have found you righteous in this generation." (Genesis 6:22–7:1)

Noah continued to build the ark for many years despite how ridiculous it looked to friends, family, and the public. The difference between making a decision and accepting an instruction is that you are the senior partner on the task or project at hand. Your actions are motivated by a resolve within you to tow that path required to achieve your destiny. You must have the conviction that your course of action is good. Divine assignments are often born out of exercising your God-given willpower to accept a truth and live it for the rest of your life. In it, you have agreed that your circumstances will change for every step you take. It starts a learning process that ultimately surrenders to your purpose in life but gradually becomes less about you and all about God. At this point in your life, the truth confronts you, forcing you to make a decision to embrace something you do not recognize but find authentic and critical to survival. There will be no need to consult friends and family; rather, you'll be informing them of the manifestation of something new in your life. Noah decided to do everything God commanded him in Genesis 6, and his divine assignment manifested for him and his generation in Genesis 7. Have you been struggling with the truth and promptings in your spirit, enduring cycles of affliction, simply because you have refused to obey and accept your true calling?

The woman with the issue of blood said to herself, "If only I can touch the helm of His garment, I'll be made whole." Jabez realized the difficulty in his life and cried out to God to bless him and enlarge his territory (1 Chronicles 4:9–10). The prodigal son came to his senses, decided to return home, and asked for his father's forgiveness. Jonah found himself in a dilemma while running away from God's assignment, begged to be thrown into the sea, entered the belly of a fish for three days, and ultimately accepted his divine task. Naomi lost her husband and two sons and then made the decision to return to her homeland where God was blessing her people. Hannah received counsel from the priest and then decided she would cry no more for the fruit of the womb. Your circumstance might not be in an atmosphere of distress. After all, the woman at the well in Samaria (John 4) recognized her situation only when Christ revealed the truth of her lifestyle in a meek and loving way. Mary, the mother of Jesus Christ, was engaged to be married when a divine conversation made her accept a decision that would change the course of her life forever. Joshua was in an ultimate position of power and leadership of God's chosen people, but in recognition of the move and faithfulness of God, he made a declaration that would consecrate his family and impact generations for God forever. So wherever you currently enjoy perceived peace and life is a positive; however, a divine encounter could change everything, bringing you to that decision point—what do you do when your life shifts in an unexpected direction and you see yourself being drawn to make a decision for God. No matter the situation, one thing is certain: God will be present in those divine moments when your assignment is being revealed as the anchor to your glorious destiny and the altar of that divine decision. He is watching over His word to perform it in your life (Jeremiah 1:12). Your role on that stage is to make a decision for God. That moment becomes your testimony in Christ, the basis for your victory in life because the Bible says that we overcome by the word of our testimony (Revelation 12:11).

Your decision is your access to your divine assignment. It is the beginning of a lifetime where you have to trust God to take you to your purpose. It starts a lifelong learning process into the demonstration and things of God. You begin to operate in the supernatural, listening for the voice of God and obeying because you trust God about the good thing He has begun in your life. It is not an easy phase of life. Definitely, most people miss their divine appointments at this point, when the allure of the world or the deceptions of evil forces cause them to deny themselves that privilege. That moment of truth will ultimately become the foundation, the altar, where your divine assignment unfolds or expands to the glory of God. You alone can make that decision to trust Him to reveal the truth about your destiny. God allowed His only begotten Son to die for your salvation. That decision changed everything and redeemed us from the curse of the law. Prayer and living a life of holiness and righteousness creates the environment that will give you the assurance you desire.

So your decision is critical to accepting and operating in your divine assignment. How can you conquer this moment and build your altar as a memorial to God?

1. Research the Promise

> Then Joshua son of Nun secretly sent two spies from Shittim. "Go, look over the land," he said, "especially Jericho." So they went and entered the house of a prostitute named Rahab and stayed there. (Joshua 2:1)

Unusual feelings and events are signs that you have come into your journey. This would often trigger a prompting that could be mistaken for restlessness and trouble. Beneath these sensations lies the innate nature of man to look for assurances. You should prayerfully research your promise. This could be through prayer, studying God's Word, or attending Holy Spirit-inspired events either physically or through listening to messages. It could also be seeking counsel from a true servant of God. Nicodemus sought Jesus Christ in the night to ask what he must do to possess his promise. Right there Jesus revealed the terms of reference for entering the kingdom of God. Except a man be born again he cannot enter the kingdom of God (John 3). Zacchaeus was so curious about the move of Jesus Christ amongst the people that he took a risk and climbed a tree in order to see clearly. God recognized and identified with his quest by visiting his house. That triggered repentance and salvation that was also financially profitable to his community, as he promised to return excesses he had charged as a tax collector. Eli advised Samuel on how to respond to God's voice after the third call. Caleb and Joshua's conviction after they spied on the Promised Land guaranteed them a gift that even their mentor, Moses, could not access. God delights in revealing Himself to His people. It makes Him so happy!

2 Seek Confirmation in Prayer

> But Abram said, "O Sovereign LORD, how can I know that
> I will gain possession of it?" (Genesis 15:8)

You can ask God to confirm what you've heard or the promptings in your spirit before embarking on your assignment. After Abraham requested God's confirmation, he slept in the process, but God still showed up and consumed the offering he had placed at the altar as a confirmation of His word and reiterated His divine covenant with Abraham (Gen. 15:8–21). Sometimes, you may not receive a response in all circumstances because God would also expect you to exercise your faith and trust Him completely. Moses did not receive confirmation that he would deliver the people of Israel despite his attempts to identify with them, causing him to commit murder in the first instance and become a fugitive, but God showed up as a burning bush forty years later to deliver that confirmation. He preserved Moses for a greater assignment: to deliver a nation rather than individuals in conflict with one another. David received confirmation at a young age when he was anointed in front of his brothers, yet the trials he faced could have made him doubt that calling multiple times as he went through intense trials and tribulations. In-depth study and meditation will reveal David's heart as he trusted God to watch over him. The test is a sign of the level of assignment on your life.

3. Resolve Your Doubts

> Gideon replied, "If now I have found favor in your eyes,
> give me a sign that it is really you talking to me." (Judges
> 6:17)

Gideon had his doubts, so he asked for confirmation twice, and on the third call, he asked for a sign and then backed up his conviction with an offering. Three times he requested for different signs in order to be sure of the great assignment God had given him. James 1:4 says, "Perseverance must finish its work so that you may be mature and complete, not lacking anything." One of the beautiful attributes of God is that He remains faithful even when we are faithless. Thomas, a disciple of Jesus Christ, refused to accept that Jesus Christ had risen until Jesus Christ showed up and asked him to physically touch His body that was wounded for our transgressions—a sign of love and God's commitment not to lose one his own to unbelief.

Zechariah asked the angel in Luke 1:18, "How can I be sure of this? I am an old man and my wife is well along in years." He was made dumb until the promise manifested because even as a priest of God, he did not believe the angel Gabriel's message informing him that God had heard his prayer and Elizabeth, his wife, would bear a son (Luke 1:11–25). God accommodates His righteous ones and seeks to deliver them out of their troubles and anxieties. Trouble here speaks to lack of peace of mind because you are anxious to confirm the promise. Remember, the Word says that we should be anxious for nothing and in all things make supplication to God with all thanksgiving. (Philippians 4:6). Don't remain in unbelief once you have seen this evidence.

4. Total Submission to the Will of God

> "I am the Lord's servant," Mary answered. "May it be to
> me as you have said." Then the angel left her. (Luke 1:38)

None of the things we discussed earlier will obstruct your divine destiny more than your lack of total submission to the will of God for your life. Living a life without God is like buying a carton of goods without the contents. You have worked for the money to buy a desired item, only to get to the store and purchase an empty vessel. The joy in using the contents is lost without the substance. You cannot exist without the Holy Spirit. Just like Mary, the mother of Jesus in Luke 1, you must accept your divine assignment with your whole body, soul, mind, and spirit. You must be ready to forsake all in order to achieve your divine assignment and receive your gift. Mary traveled through many cities and was helped by both men and angels to achieve her purpose of giving birth to God's Son and our Savior, Jesus Christ. She did not care about the shame of carrying what seemed like a strange pregnancy, but rather, she was focused and totally submitted to God. God took over and even began to speak to Joseph, her husband, on how to support her, which helped Joseph to achieve God's purpose for his life. God is more interested in what you have inside of you than anyone else, not even your family, well-wishers, or you, because He will watch over the seed He planted in His word until it is fulfilled. But it requires total submission and surrender for you to receive your gift of infertility.

5. Don't Look Back

> When my life was ebbing away, I remembered you, LORD,
> and my prayer rose to you, to your holy temple. (Jonah 2:7)

Luke 9:62 clearly states, "No one who puts his hand to the plow and looks back is fit for service in the kingdom of God." Jonah tried to escape his divine mission and ended up in the belly of fish. Within those three days, he did everything he could have done in the first place before refusing his divine assignment, which was to explore the promise, resolve his doubts, and seek for confirmation. He had been chosen and made aware of it by God. Running away was not an option, so immediately he repented and the Lord commanded the fish to vomit Jonah onto dry land (Jonah 2:10). Lot's wife was rescued by God but missed her evil and debased world of sin so much that she rejected the counsel to move forward and looked back. She became a pillar of salt, a symbol of an object without movement or purpose. As a pillar, it was not beautiful or edifying to behold, as a human being, she no longer had life in her, and as salt in that form, it was not useful to the world. Jesus said that we are the salt of the world (Matthew 5:13), which means unleashing our assignment to the benefit of our community and the glory to God. A pinch of salt makes a difference in the family's meal but too much salt spoils the food. According to verse 13, "It is no longer good for anything except to be thrown out and trampled by men."

Elisha was determined not to look back and followed Elijah to Gilgal, Bethel, Jericho, and Jordan, even after Elijah had told him to go back three times. Elisha was consumed by the divine assignment ahead of him and displayed a sense of urgency. As soon as he received the mantle, he used it immediately to part the river of Jordan, a demonstration of his decision to activate his divine assignment immediately and move forward.

What about you? What have you done with the mantle you received?

CHAPTER 5

Divine Connections

So Jeremiah called Baruch son of Neriah, and while
Jeremiah dictated all the words the Lord had spoken to
him, Baruch wrote them on the scroll. (Jeremiah 36:4)

I n Genesis 2, God said, "It is not good for man to be alone." In the same
chapter, He delegated a divine task to man to name every living creature.
Adam did not need a lifetime of study, many years of work experience,
or multiple professional qualifications as requirement to perform this
divine task. The disciples possessed no qualifications directly related to
the assignment to which they were called. All you need is the presence
of the Lord in your life. In fulfilling your divine assignment, God always
sends destiny helpers and divine connections. Your spouse could be one
of them. This could also be either an angel (a heavenly messenger) or a
fellow human being sent to assist you and give you a sense of direction
and purpose. "For he will command his angels concerning you to guard
you in all your ways" (Psalm 91:11). God sent the angel Gabriel to Mary,
the mother of our Lord and Savior, Jesus Christ, to give her details of her
assignment. An angel was also sent to inform Zechariah about the birth of
John the Baptist. Therefore, it is possible for you to encounter an angel in
a dream or in real life. "Are not all angels ministering spirits sent to serve
those who will inherit salvation?" (Hebrews 1:14).

In other cases in the Bible, and in most people's lives, the Lord God
used another human being to bless, inform, inspire, or activate their

divine assignment. This could be a direct instruction, prophecy, or a new door of opportunity. Sometimes it requires the help of the Holy Spirit to discern what you are expected to do. Other times you need to take baby steps of faith before God can release the nature of the assignment or your divine destiny as you mature. In rare cases, some people get clear and explicit instructions through dreams, visions, visitations, and supernatural encounters. Abraham had a divine visitation from strangers, which some versions of the Bible also called angels. Manoah's wife had a divine visitation from an angel who they both mistook for an ordinary man. He told her that she was going to give birth to a son (Samson) who was to be a Nazirite, dedicated to God from the womb (Judges 13). He was to deliver Israel from the Philistines.

Paul had a supernatural encounter with the Lord on his way to Damascus that changed the course of his life forever. Joseph, the husband of Mary, the mother of Jesus Christ, received most divine instructions through dreams. Jacob had a vision, which led to the struggle with an angel that changed his life and name forever. In our text above, the collaboration between Baruch and the prophet Jeremiah is a clear case of God sending a divine helper and a divine connection. They both needed each other to achieve their divine task. Your ability to recognize an event, activity, or person as a divine connection depends a lot on you as an individual and your spiritual state.

When God wanted to rescue a nation and deliver the people to their promised land, he also assigned a servant of God who listened for His voice. In Exodus 14:16, God said to Moses, "Raise your staff and stretch out your hand over the sea to divide the water so that the Israelites can go through the sea on dry ground." This man or woman becomes the divine helper for a people and a divine connection to anyone willing to serve God under him or her. Out of the multitudes of people that came out of Egypt, Joshua and Caleb remained faithful and were rewarded with divine assignments and gifts of infertility.

Positioning Yourself to Make Divine Connections

1. Positive Disposition

> And Ruth the Moabite said to Naomi, "Let me go to the fields and pick up the leftover grain behind anyone in whose eyes I find favor." Naomi said to her, "Go ahead, my daughter." (Ruth 2:2)

Maintain a positive disposition by making yourself and your environment receptive physically and spiritually to both people and the Holy Spirit. You cannot be attractive when you are always frowning, worrying, angry, antagonistic, bitter, or complaining. Human beings wouldn't even want to be around you, let alone the holy and divine presence of God. These behaviors are sinful in themselves and elicit sinful responses from others, which is double trouble for you! In Matthew 6, Jesus said, "Your worrying cannot affect anything." Complaining will only distract your destiny helpers and may generate anger that will affect both your assignments. How often have you seen yourself achieving your destiny or taking steps toward it and it never materializes? How often do you experience "near success syndrome," "almost there" moments and failure at the edge of your breakthrough? While many reasons can be responsible for this affliction, your disposition to divine connections could be the problem. Other manifestations of a negative disposition are bad temperament, ingratitude, and pride. If you find that people who have helped you are now uncomfortable around you, stop and ask yourself sincere questions. Try to nip it at the bud before it ruins your life. Also, remember that the wealth of the wicked is stored up for the righteous, so that person you want to get rid of might be storing up your wealth of knowledge, property, and other blessings for you. He or she could be the divine access to your testimony. It was a maid that spoke to her master's wife about a prophet before Nathan got his healing. Don't be in a hurry to write people off. Simply commit everything to God in prayer. He alone understands you and what you are going through and has the master plan for your destiny.

2. Let Go of All Forms of Unforgiveness and Malice

> The Lord within her is righteous; he does no wrong. Morning by morning he dispenses his justice, and every new day he does not fail, yet the unrighteous know no shame. (Zephaniah 3:5)

Unforgiveness and malice exempts you from true worship and robs you of God's presence. How then can you discern and seek His face if you cannot approach the throne of grace in spirit and in truth? Living in unforgiveness and malice simply means that you have given the other party the authority to keep you in bondage and ultimately send you to hell. The one you are angry at may have moved on and surrendered completely to Christ while you are still rehearsing your hurt and having pity parties. How can you achieve your destiny with such a troubled soul and a life full of darkness? You cannot drive a car forward while focusing on the rearview mirror. The end result will be a crash that could be fatal. No matter your level of expertise, you may try, but it will be a short-lived exercise. The risk in the adventure cannot be overemphasized: calamity and possibly death, in this case, spiritual death. It is undeniable that you may have been hurt seriously, painfully, and grievously. Jesus Christ Himself went through torture and anguish but ended on a note of forgiveness even while He was dying on the cross. He was focused on His mission and no devil in hell could stop Him. He went through pain for us. He achieved His earthly mission and won His place at the right hand of God. Even if you've let another rob you of a life of joy and peace, will you also let him or her steal your crown? Don't let that happen. No one is so important to cost you your destiny. You must repent now and ask God to give you the grace to forgive those who have hurt you. Then release them to also achieve their divine assignments while you focus on your gift of infertility.

3. Be Hospitable

> If a Levite moves from one of your towns anywhere in Israel where he is living, and *comes in all earnestness to the place the Lord will choose,* he may minister in the name of the Lord his God like all his fellow Levites who serve

there in the presence of the Lord. (Deuteronomy 18:6–7, emphasis added)

Some people simply don't know how to be kind to strangers and the poor. They see them as a source of embarrassment, irritation, and distraction to their worldly status. Abraham would have missed his appointed time for his blessing if he did not reach out to welcome those strangers who turned out to be angels sent by God to proclaim his blessing and ultimately Sarah's gift of infertility (Gen. 18). Her hospitality may have even compensated for her doubt and unbelief. God rewards and watches over His word to perform it. He has the final say because His word is yea and amen. He must accomplish His purpose on earth whether you cooperate with Him or not. If your act of rebellion becomes a hindrance like in the case of King Saul, God will appoint another to complete the task. King Saul was rejected and David was anointed as king. Despite all of David's indiscretions, he was hospitable and loved God. God said in the Bible that King David was a man after His own heart. God blessed David with lineage that directly linked to His throne to Jesus Christ. Remember, a singular act of kindness from Abraham and Sarah announced their destiny and activated Sarah's gift, Isaac. And out of Isaac came the fulfillment of the manifestation of the twelve tribes of Israel. Those divine visitors were Sarah's destiny helpers and divine connection to God's promise of a child to her and Abraham.

4. Show Love and Compassion

"They will be mine," says the Lord Almighty, "in the day when I make up my treasured possession. I will spare them, just as in compassion a man spares his son who serves him. And you will again see the distinction between the righteous and the wicked, between those who serve God and those who do not." (Malachi 3:17)

The greatest commandment is to love our neighbors as ourselves. God demonstrated divine love by allowing His only begotten Son to die for our sins. Lack of love demonstrated through pride, covetousness, and selfishness has robbed many people of their destiny. Your willingness to make sacrifices for the greater good of other people, your community, or simply out of compassion also shows love. Esther's uncle and maidservants ushered in her divine assignment to save a whole nation from destruction because she was willing to make a sacrifice out of love and compassion for her people. She honored the guidance of her divine helpers and said, "If I perish, I perish" (Esther 4:16). Moses was determined to save his people, the Israelites, from Egypt, even though he went about it the wrong way. But ultimately the Lord guided him to his destiny after spending forty years in exile. This is very important. In both cases, their acts of love complemented the destiny of others, such as Modecai, Aaron, Joshua, Caleb, and the Israelites. God delights in those who serve Him in spirit and in truth by showing love as He commanded us.

5. Giving

> For God so loved the world that he gave his one and only Son, that whoever believes in him shall not perish but have eternal life. (John 3:16)

Giving is a divine act of love. You may have done everything required by God to activate your gift of infertility but still live an unfulfilled life. In some cases, your generosity is all that you require to get to the finish line. Giving comes in many forms: kindness, charity, offerings of different types, sowing seed for divine purposes, and financial gifts. The size and level of giving may or may not be relevant to your mission, but God wants to see how faithful you are in either sharing your worldly acquisition or trusting Him to make provision. The widow at Zarephath gave Elijah a meal out of a circumstance of lack (1 Kings 17:7–24), and the Shunamite woman provided accommodation for Elisha (2 Kings 4:8–17) from a situation of plenty. They gave and received their gifts of infertility. God rewarded Abraham for his disposition and willingness to give his promised son, Isaac. God Himself gave His only begotten Son, Jesus Christ, because of His love for us (John 3:16).

Oftentimes, giving that activates your destiny comes through revelation. God will use you to bless someone or a project, and other times, He prompts you to give sacrificially to test you. This is one test you cannot fail. In order to know how to give or when to give, you must seek God in prayer and obey instructions relating to periodic giving in the Bible. Also, true men of God and your spiritual parents can guide your giving through their own revelation and prayer. Don't fail to take advantage of those divine moments in the assembly of the righteous and presence of the anointing.

CHAPTER 6

The Place of Your Birthing Process

Giving orders to the people: "When you see the ark of covenant of the LORD your God, and the priests, who are Levites, carrying it, you are to move out from your position and follow it." (Joshua 3:3)

Movement and progress are essential to achieving your divine assignment. Identifying and recognizing the place for your birthing process is critical to your receiving your gift of infertility. Your willingness to discern and move out of your comfort zone is essential to your retaining and functioning in your gift. This could be short trips to diverse locations, transferring to a different department in the office, joining another ministry, or a complete relocation to a new city. You cannot afford to be stubborn about any promptings by the Holy Spirit or explicit instructions to move or take the next step toward receiving your prophetic calling that will birth your gift. You are either in one location doing different things or being asked to move for a reason. The reason may not always be evident, and you may encounter severe difficulties. But ultimately, God will reveal Himself to you at that place where you are destined to be at that time. Your divine encounter can happen either on the way to the location or at the destination. The extent to which your faith is tested depends on the size of your divine assignment. In Genesis, Joseph went from a pit to a prison before he entered the palace to possess his destiny. Daniel developed himself and acquired a spirit of excellence on his long walk to freedom. In Exodus, Moses went from a basket in the river to a palace as prince, became a fugitive, and ended up in the desert where God appeared to him. The children of Israel traveled from Egypt through the wilderness to possess the Promised Land. Jonah went from a relaxed cruise on a ship to the belly of a fish, where he spent three gruesome days before he obeyed God's call to go to Nineveh. These are biblical examples of people who achieved their destiny and received their gifts in their birthing place.

Divine Movements and Transfers

I will give you every place where you set your foot, as I promised Moses. (Joshua 1:3)

Soon after man and woman were created, God positioned them in a place called the garden of Eden. In this place, they had access to every resource available on Earth. They could have manifested all gifts in this place if sin did not corrupt their lives. Adam and Eve were subsequently sent out to work out their existence and explore their gifts in hard labor. The garden of Eden was also their place of worship and fellowship with God. Noah was preserved in a place, an ark, despite the storm and flood that wiped out humanity. God will always protect you at your divine location because He made the provision before you were born. When God called Abraham, one of the first instructions He gave him was to move to a new place. While Abraham was in transit, he became prosperous and developed his faith, and God took time to nurture a close relationship with him. He moved from one city to another, and when he got to his final destination, his gift was established. He became a symbol of God's covenant for God's chosen generation and a father of all nations. Sarah, his wife, also received the gift of a child when Isaac was born.

On the other hand, Isaac remained in a place at God's instruction despite the famine that eventually came upon the land. He was blessed abundantly. In fact, his wife Rebecca also took a journey to matrimony with him where her destiny was to be activated in their home. She became the mother of two nations that established the twelve tribes of Israel. Jacob was on the run from his brother, Esau, when he had a divine encounter in Bethel that transformed his life and gave him a new name, Israel. A similar movement activated the reconciliation with his brother as he went on take possession of his divine assignment. Joseph was sold into slavery by his brothers and transported to Egypt where he found his destiny and eventually became the prime minister and controller of the country's economy. Moses ran away from a palace to the desert to hide and was preserved for forty years for his assignment that was eventually announced through a prophetic and divine encounter with God in the burning bush. He led the children of Israel out of bondage, through the Red Sea, and into the wilderness on their journey to possess the Promised Land.

Saul, who became king, was sent on an errand to look for a missing ass when he had a divine encounter on the way that transformed his destiny. David was seated at a place in the bush when he was sought and anointed by a prophet who was sent on a journey by God to identify the new king. Elijah ran away from Jezebel despite his powerful anointing to a place where he received his next assignment. Elisha followed Elijah around from one city to another to receive a double portion of his anointing. Jonah was transported in the belly of a fish for three days in order to fulfill an assignment. Mary and Joseph moved from place to place to protect their gift and assignment. Jesus Christ moved from one city to another throughout His childhood and ministry for His entire assignment to be fulfilled. The disciples went everywhere with Jesus to learn and master their assignment. They received their prophetic calling in a location called the upper room when they had an encounter with the Holy Spirit and their gifts exploded. The disciples then went from one place to another to demonstrate the power in the gospel of Jesus Christ. Our Lord and Savior, Jesus Christ, went through fourteen stations of the cross to seal his divine assignment at Calvary. Paul was on his way to destroy Christians when he had a divine encounter with God at a location called Damascus. He traveled throughout his ministry to establish his divine destiny. The Acts of the Apostles manifested throughout their many travels and missionary journeys.

When God decides that you need to be in a place for your gift to manifest, you must obey the call. Any reluctance or delay on your part will simply add more years to your waiting period. You might spend time praying, fasting, and casting and binding the devil over a change in your heart's desire, but until you obey the prophetic call at a place destined for you, you're just wasting your time. My spiritual father once said that some people living and struggling abroad are actually destined to be people of great influence in politics, business, and ministry in their home countries. But they prefer to live abroad than to work out their destiny in their birthing place. Similarly, some people have simply refused to relocate abroad due to family sentiments and attachments to temporal things of the world. They are local champions when they are destined to be world changers, trendsetters, and history makers. You might remain in one company on staff for many years when obeying a simple call could have made you a CEO of a larger organization. Similarly, you may have been jumping from one company to another when you could have been rapidly promoted to a position of influence if you had stayed longer at one of those organizations.

As you can see, place and movement are essential to your birthing process. Your ministry might be currently located in the wrong city or country. Identifying the place of your birthing process is as important as the gift itself. In the Bible, Ruth moved to find her Boaz and achieved her divine assignment, which earned her a position in the genealogy of Jesus Christ. What an honor to a woman who lost all but trusted God and made a commitment to follow her mother-in-law, Naomi, to a new location. It was Ruth's place for her birthing process, but Naomi's destination for her gift of infertility. You cannot afford to remain in your comfort zone or be stubborn about any promptings for you to move and take the next step. You are here for a reason, which must be fulfilled. The circumstances around you, fear of leaving family behind, mode of transportation, geographical location, or even being driven/chased out against your will is irrelevant. When God decides that you need to be in a place for your destiny to manifest, you must obey. Resistance is an act of rebellion, and God does not like rebellious people. However, God is faithful and patient enough to help you get to your divine location. The most important thing is for your steps to be guided by God. You must discern and activate the process where you can actually know where your gift will manifest.

CHAPTER 7

Access Your Divine Gift

The company of the prophets said to Elisha, "Look, the
place where we meet with you is too small for us. Let us
go to the Jordan, where each of us can get a pole; and let
us build a place there for us to live." And he said, "Go."
(2 Kings 6:1–2)

In our opening text, the company of prophets were individuals who had
moved into their divine position for advancement within the kingdom
of God. They had actually developed themselves, earned the title of
prophet, and had close access to a powerful man of God, Elisha. They
were passionate about their divine assignment and supportive of Elisha's
mission, so they sought expansion of their physical and spiritual location.
Access to your priest, pastor, general overseer, or the religious is a privilege
yet requires the right motive to bear fruit. If your closeness to God's servant
does not support your spiritual growth, you should do a self reexamination.
What are you really laboring for? Are you in the right location? Is that a
divine connection? A true servant of God will discern any wrong motives
and will not take advantage of this weakness in you by using you for
manual labor or financial gain without consideration for your advancement
within the kingdom of God. He or she would rather work with you and
mentor you to achieve your potential. These prophets had the desire, and
Elisha must have been waiting for them to mature and get to this point
where they recognized the need for expansion and promotion so he could

take them to the next level. His only response to their request was "Go." Short and precise. On their second request for him to come with them, he simply replied, "I will" (v. 3).

A true servant of God can teach you by his conduct without speaking many words. The aim is to support and move you to your next level while allowing you to move at your own pace. If the movement is too slow, he could do something sudden or drastic to accelerate your promotion within the hierarchy. Elijah did this to Elisha when he threw his mantle on him. Elisha was busy with his day job when all of a sudden Elijah walked by and changed his destiny. Elisha also surrendered all and followed him, a sign of his total commitment to and readiness for his divine assignment. If you've been waiting faithfully in service to God, you cannot miss that opportunity. Elijah subsequently fired him three times at Gilgal, Bethel, and Jericho, yet Elisha refused to leave him alone. For his tenacity, resilience, and devotion, Elisha received a double portion of his master's anointing. Elisha was said to have done even more miracles than his master and mentor, Elijah.

Your enthusiasm and initiative guided by the Holy Spirit will show your seriousness about the things of God. Light cannot be hidden. Money cannot buy this for you. No amount of seed sowing can guarantee this level of access and success. Once you have opened yourself up to be used by God, things may or may not move quickly, but you'll surely reap what you sow. Joshua worked under Moses for many years before he received his divine assignment to take the children of Israel to the Promised Land (Deuteronomy 31:23). Jacob's training process was working for his father-in-law for fourteen years under deceptive circumstances. But he ultimately received a reward. It all depends on the nature of the task God has designed for you to do; therefore, do not be afraid to make mistakes and shout out when you have derailed, backslid, or failed. You may or may not require co-laborers to complete your task like the company of prophets, but be rest assured that God will back you up with His might (Psalm 37:23–24). In the corporate world, you find that most departments consist of teams as well as individual contributors. Be sensitive to the nature of your assignment and how God desires to use you. Do not envy or be jealous of other people's path to success or level of achievement; it will only contaminate your progress, slow you down, and ultimately derail you if you do not seek help.

In 2 Kings 6:5–7, one of the prophets dropped his key implement for the task and cried out for help. Elisha immediately responded by using a very simple solution to solve the problem. Oftentimes, we are overwhelmed and distracted by what seems like an enormous challenge, but God has placed spiritual authority over us to assist and counsel us. Most people who have had similar challenges supported those who did or are instructed by God on how to handle it in order to ensure that your divine assignment is carried out and protected. Once again, Elisha did not say much to him in order to bring healing, deliverance, and progress back into this man's life. The man also confessed his inadequacies by mentioning his failure and how he acquired the tool. "It was borrowed!" (2 Kings 6:5) he said. This demonstrates that we need to pick up, borrow, and learn from others in order to advance to our divine destiny. A simple invitation by someone to attend a Christian event or watching a Christian channel on television might be the turning point in your life. You can also achieve this through Holy Spirit-inspired books, teachings, and CDs, and DVDs by truly anointed servants of God. If you are led, it could be useful to learn from sources outside your immediate servitude or place of worship because the Bible says, "Iron sharpenth Iron." (Proverbs 27:17) But be careful not to get entangled with false teaching. It is your responsibility to move from being a spiritual baby to the level of maturity required for your gift to manifest. Once you have accepted your divine assignment, He will give you wisdom and supernatural abilities to perform the task. Anyone challenging your divine assignment will be fighting God.

Receiving Your Gift of Infertility

> Behold, I am coming soon! My reward is with me, and I will give to everyone according to what he has done. I am the Alpha and the Omega, the First and the Last, the Beginning and the End. (Revelation 22:12–13)

At the appointed time, when you start hearing God's footsteps and voice concerning your divine assignment, you begin to train yourself to accept His ultimate purpose for your life. This new experience is not devoid of new levels of battles and spiritual attacks, for the Bible says, "Many are

the afflictions of the righteous but the Lord delivers them from it all."
(Psalm 34:19). You may have spent time with God or started to serve Him
diligently in a ministry or under an anointed man of God, but nothing
prepares you for your initial reaction when that ultimate call comes. Your
initial reaction to receiving your promise is unpredictable. You may have
done all yet be stricken by an unexpected reaction and shock when the gift
or nature of your divine assignment finally manifests. It does not depend
on your age, preparedness, education, experience, or spiritual maturity.
This is why a true child of God is truly a child *before* God. In real life,
children react unexpectedly to gifts from friends and family. The Bible
constantly refers to us as children, and as we continue to seek God and
desire to know him more, He is ever willing to reveal Himself to us as
our Father and set the stage for our unique gift of infertility to be made
manifest to the world.

Looking at biblical examples, children of promise were called and
chosen in different ways and their diverse gifts revealed in distinct ways.
Saul had a zeal channeled at the wrong mission of killing and persecuting
Christians until he encountered the Lord on his way to Damascus. His
name was subsequently changed to Paul, and he began to fellowship in
the company of the faithful. All the disciples were in different professions,
including fishing and finance, until Jesus Christ called them to follow
Him. Joseph's gift of dreams lifted him from the pit to the palace. David
was a shepherd when he was anointed king and ultimately started the
lineage of Jesus Christ.

Your experience would most likely be different from another child of
promise. Do not compete but rather share experiences and rejoice with
each other, always giving God all the glory and honor. There is no basis for
competition. We all have different gifts and have been assigned to different
tasks. You must focus on the goal and forsake all distractions. When it
is time to possess your possession, to receive your gift of infertility, God
displays an enthusiasm to show you the magnitude of the promise He has
in store for you. That is the beauty and faithfulness of God. In all this,
He often gives instructions on the supernatural steps you must take to
secure your gift. Joshua 1 gives a summary of the steps that ended years
of wandering and how he led the children of Israel to victory and into the
Promised Land—their gift of infertility.

CHAPTER 8

Eternal Gifts of Infertility

This is what the LORD says—he who made you, who formed you in the womb, and who will help you: Do not be afraid ... whom I have chosen. For I will pour water on the thirsty land, and streams on the dry ground; I will pour out my Spirit on your offspring and my blessing on your descendants. (Isaiah 44:2–3)

God gave us many gifts borne out of infertility in certain areas of creation. These gifts are freely given to assist our existence on earth and journey through life as we walk with God in our divine assignments toward achieving our specific gifts of infertility. Three distinct gifts of God given to humanity.

1. The work of your hands
2. The gift of children
3. The gift of eternal life

The Work of Your Hands

Moreover, when God gives any man wealth and possessions, and enables him to enjoy them, to accept his lot and be happy in his work—this a gift of God. (Ecclesiastes 5:19)

Man was created in the image of God. God's intention was for man to be fertile in all areas of life. The first reference to fertility started with a command from God for man to be fruitful and multiply. Thereafter, man was sent off to the garden of Eden to enjoy what God had already laid out for us. Sin came into the lives of Adam and Eve, and they lost fellowship with God. Another reference to God's commitment to His mandate was after the destruction of the world by flood. He wanted to recreate the earth through Noah and his family, the only ones who were saved. God commanded them once again to be fruitful and multiply. Despite the fall of man, God in many verses in the Bible reiterated that none shall be barren in the land. In other words, there was no interruption to the process of fertility and fruitfulness except by divine authorization from God and for His glory. Fertility manifests as fruitfulness in all areas of our lives. Being fruitful refers to birth, growth, creativity, productivity, innovation, and expansion. Despite this mandate given to man, we find that a major problem with humanity is infertility in various areas of our lives.

Man was created in God's image so he became a carrier of God's creativity and endowed with the gift of His recreating abilities. In Jeremiah 1, He said "Before you were formed, I knew you." You have been deposited with the potential to create and manifest your destiny, which will bear fruit and trigger other divine assignments. It is more painful for a gift not to fulfill its purpose, which is why God rebukes people who run away from their assignment. This is why Jonah found himself in the belly of the fish and Samson lost his eyes to his enemies. And Saul became mad and the prodigal son fed with pigs. No matter how painful the process, God's thoughts for us are good. This is also why any company that focuses on its human resources always outlives many generations. History never forgets great men and women who have impacted lives and raised future leaders. Every speech made by those of the younger generation starts with a mention of their source of inspiration or mentor, giving honor to whom honor is due. God commanded us to be fruitful and multiply without pronouncing our specific gifts at birth so we can work out our salvation. The earth is waiting for the manifestation of the sons of God who will bless generations. We are waiting for you to manifest your gift and take center stage in achieving God's purpose.

Unfortunately, we spend time doing everything else, seeking our heart desires and the material things of this world without stopping to ask if we are really working/walking in our divine calling. When you see a man, ministry, or nation operating in its divine domain, everything is fruitful and multiplies. It is imperative that you identify your gift and desire to operate within your gift. It has nothing to do with education, social status, or worldly possessions. It requires no application, protocol, or connections. When you are in the will of God and operating in your gift, people of influence will want to be identified with you. Gifts and wealth just come to you. Matthew 6:33 says, "But seek first his kingdom and his righteousness, and all these things will be given to you as well."

The world is quick to celebrate and magnify blessings, but how anointed and prophetic is the object producing the blessing? Any factory or person can produce, but during economic recession or life's struggles, only people, businesses, ministries, and nations that are set apart for a divine purpose will outlive the crises. This is why people rise and fall, excel today and fail tomorrow. This is why people can walk into unimaginable wealth and lose everything within a short time. This is why one can marry an angel and treat his or her spouse like the devil himself. This is why you can have covenant children at home and leave them at the mercy of domestic staff to bully and train them. This is why people can have their dream job and still spend time gossiping and lamenting about how the company is not taking care of staff welfare. This is why a church ministry would deceive its members and focus on money rather than preaching the undiluted Word of God. This is why a charity worker would sell products meant for the poor instead of giving it to them for free. This is why nations with abundant human and natural resources are still borrowing, lack basic infrastructure, and good leadership. This is why people can stick to fruitless religious beliefs/practices and live in spiritual blindness in the presence of the gospel truth. The Pharisees and Sadducees where still quoting the law even when they were right in front of grace, the Messiah, the Lord God Himself.

Are you lacking in the fruit of your labor, land, investment, and knowledge? You may already have a vision of your gift, but are you focused on developing and receiving your gift or simply waiting for a blessing? Your gift and other blessings may be complementary but are mutually exclusive. Your gift requires a level of maturity to nurture and execute God's divine assignment. Your gift gives you a solid background to take care of your blessings. Your gift is the foundation required for your stable and fulfilling existence on earth. Your inability to distinguish between the two and discern the true source of a blessing could create additional problems in your future. "The blessings of God maketh rich and added no sorrow." (Proverbs 10:22). If you are in crisis, you still haven't found your gift. Embrace God's gift in Genesis 1:28, and live a life of fulfillment.

The Gift of Children

> Behold, children are a heritage from the LORD. The fruit
> of the womb is His reward. (Psalm 127:3 NKJV)

In Genesis, the first mention of infertility in the Bible starts with Adam and Eve's punishment where God pronounced hard labor and difficult childbearing upon them yet did not alter his command for them to be fruitful and multiply. The second mention was the manifestation of infertility in the bodies of Abraham and Sarah. Sarah waited and gave birth to a child at age eighty, the child of promise (Galatians 4:28), which became her gift of infertility. The gift of children is God's way of regenerating His image on earth—birthing something with the potential and capability to recreate and operate in a divine assignment. This is also why God has repeatedly said and proven to us that "none shall be barren," including animals and vegetation. God uses this gifting process in the womb, the birth of a child, to achieve divine assignments on earth and ultimate purpose for humanity. He cannot afford for this process to be interrupted.

Notice that grown carnal man is not a gift, but the Bible says that children are a gift from God. God loves to refer to us as children because of our spiritual blessings in Christ (Ephesians 1:5) and our earthly heritage as followers of God (Ephesians 5:1). In Luke 18:15–17, the disciples rebuked people bringing their babies to Jesus to bless them. But He said to them, "Let the little children come to me, and do not hinder them, for the kingdom of God belongs to *such as* these. I tell you the truth, anyone who will not receive the kingdom of God *like* a little child will never enter it" (emphasis added). To walk into your destiny, you have to unlearn all the ungodly tendencies you have picked up from the world and humble yourself at the feet of Christ like a child in order to receive your gift of infertility.

Abraham's heart's desire was to have an heir, but God's plan was to establish a covenant and make Abraham the father of all nations. Abraham attempted to obtain his heart's desire himself by birthing Ishmael through Sarah's maidservant, which created untold strife and distraction. Our God is not a God of confusion, so that was evidence that it was not His plan for Abraham's destiny. God mercifully intervened and protected Abraham's divine assignment amidst the chaos and ultimately created a generation through his seed by a covenant. Can you imagine what could have happened if Abraham wasn't faithful or if God had withdrawn His mercy? An entire part of the Bible story may have been nonexistent with no mention of what became of Abraham, his generation, and our role model on how to live a life of faith. Perhaps God would have raised another person, but Abraham's gift, his legacy, would have been lost and forgotten.

God always acknowledged that Abraham would bear children at the appointed time. Sarah's fruit was important to God; therefore, the process took time and defied all human expectations because this seed was a special gift of infertility to humanity. Delay in childbearing is not a denial but part of a divine plan to bless a generation through you. God demonstrates the pricelessness of the fruit of the womb as a gift, especially for His chosen vessels Sarah, Mary, Hannah, Rebekah, Rachel, and Elizabeth. Your child is precious in God's eyes.

The Gift of Eternal Life

> Blessed are those who wash their robes, that they may have the right to the tree of life and may go through the gates into the city. (Revelation 22:14)

God promised eternal life before the beginning of time (Titus 1:2). The garden of Eden was a reflection of God's intention for man to live and fellowship with Him. After the fall of man in the garden of Eden, God wanted to reconcile us to Himself through a divine promise unrevealed until many years later. Our reconciliation was essential to fulfilling our destiny and recovering our gifts of infertility. Man fell to sin and was driven out into a life of making decisions between good and evil, a dilemma that often introduces all sorts of infertility in life when the wrong decisions are made. Throughout the Old Testament, God used mediators, laws, and commandments to set standards for His people, but they remained rebellious and sinful. In the New Testament, the death and resurrection of Jesus Christ gave us access to the throne of grace through prayer in His name. This began a journey into eternal life, a life by the Spirit. Unfortunately, most people remain cursed because they are still stuck in observing the law (Galatians 3), depriving them of living by the Spirit and reaping eternal life (Galatians 6:8). Jesus acknowledged in Matthew 19:26 that this might seem impossible, but not with God. A life by the Spirit bears fruit as evidence of inheritance of the divine love of God the Father, God the Son, and God the Holy Spirit. Eternal life abides in you, and you are a joint heir with Christ according to His mercy and grace (Titus 3:7). God desires to bring you back into fellowship and relationship with Him. The Holy Spirit, the counselor, will provide all you need to achieve your divine assignment. He will give you divine direction, empower you, position divine helpers, bring you to the right locations, and provide the right learning opportunities required for your growth and access to spiritual authority that will mentor you. The gift of God is eternal life in Christ Jesus our Lord (Romans 6:22–23), and it is free.

CHAPTER 9

Source of All Gifts of Infertility

But the scripture declares that the whole world is a prisoner of sin, so that what was promised, being given through faith in Jesus Christ, might be given to those who believe. (Galatians 3:22)

In all communication with Abraham, God always focused on Abraham's destiny while Abraham was initially focused on his childlessness. God developed His friendship with Abraham through a spiritual birthing process and then established His covenant as a generational gift to Abraham. "You shall be my people and I shall be your God." (Jeremiah 30:22). Abraham was chosen to be the father of all nations, a destiny that had been established before his heir was born. He had to be carefully launched into his divine purpose and destiny, which would impact generations to come. Although both the covenant and Isaac were gifts, God wanted to first build a relationship and develop these vessels (Abraham and Sarah) because His plan for their lives was beyond just having a child like everyone around them. This gift had to be the heir to the Abrahamic blessing, the basis for the salvation available to both Jews and Gentiles, the core of our initiation into a life with God and ultimately through Jesus Christ.

Genesis 15 records the promise that God gave to humanity through Abraham during this conversation on fertility. This promise is the anchor to receiving any gift of infertility in your life. The promise was embedded in the covenant with Abraham as the seed of reconciliation with humanity.

Abram believed because he had faith that God who said it was faithful to perform it. Genesis 15:6 tells us, "Abraham believed the LORD, and he credited it to him as righteousness." The substance of the promise was evident, but the actual evidence was yet to be revealed. The actual evidence was Jesus Christ, yet Abraham caught the revelation and believed God by faith. Righteousness by faith is the prerequisite for receiving your gift of infertility. You must have faith in God to believe the promise for your life. Believing in Jesus Christ is not lip service but a resolve within you to trust against all odds that you'll receive God's promise for your life. Abraham maintained right standing before God and demonstrated complete faith in God, which was credited to him as righteousness. He maintained a life of worship and total surrender to the will of God despite his shortcomings and temptations. Therefore, your countenance while you are waiting should reflect this same revelation.

Your Belief System

> For God so loved the world that he gave his one and only Son, that *whoever believes* in him shall not perish but have eternal life. For God did not send his Son into the world to condemn the world, but to save the world through him. *Whoever believes* in him is not condemned, but *whoever does not believe* stands condemned already because he has believed in the name of God's only begotten Son. (John 3:16–18, emphasis added)

The promise only belongs to "whoever believes." It's not for everyone. You might aspire to receive your gift of infertility, but the starting point rests in your belief system. The source of all gifts is Jesus Christ, and the emphasis is on whoever believes. Do you believe?

God's love for humanity was demonstrated by His giving of His only begotten Son to save our relationship with Him. Our Lord and Savior Jesus Christ's love for us was demonstrated through giving up His life to save us from sin. Acts of love and selfless giving should drive every child of God with a destiny to fulfill. God wanted to protect His investment in creation, so He shared His love to win us back and set us on the right path to achieve our divine destiny. Christ gave up His life out of love in order to free us from sin and protect our divine mandate. Having rescued us, He also sent us the Holy Spirit to guide us through the journey of fulfilling our divine assignment. In a process of love and giving, great sacrifices were made to protect us from the wrath of God (Romans 5:9) and save a mandate issued at creation but lost in the garden of Eden. A divine mandate so great that God remained committed and faithful to His promise, even depositing His Holy Spirit as our helper and counselor to prevent us from missing the mark again. This divine mandate was issued in Genesis 1:27–28 before the fall of man and immediately after God created male and female in the image of God: "And God blessed them and God said unto them, "Be fruitful and multiply, and replenish the earth, and subdue it: and have dominion over the fish of the sea, and over the fowl of the air, and over every living thing that moveth upon the earth."

The mandate sets the tone for our gift of infertility. Little wonder when man fell the judgment and punishment God pronounced for the female and male were directly related to our productivity on the earth. To the woman in Genesis 3:16 was pronounced infertility of the body (womb) and marriage: "I will greatly increase your pains in childbearing; with pain you will give birth to children. Your desire will be for your husband, and he will rule over you." To the man in Genesis 3:17 was the pronouncement of infertility of the work of his hands, represented today by career, labor, and investments: "Cursed is the ground because of you: through painful toil you will eat of it all the days of your life."

The ultimate impact was on their soul, family, nation, and ministry, leading to the loss of their divine assignments and gifts. They became naked—a state of shame, insecurity, lack, fear, and poverty. They were banished from the garden of Eden to prevent them from reaching their hands and taking also from the Tree of Life (Genesis 3:22). Humanity still groans under the burden of that judgment; hence, prevalent unfruitfulness and infertility of various forms. Eating from the Tree of Life would have made them live forever, a privilege now reserved for "whosoever believes in Jesus Christ."

Where Do *You* Stand?

For it is by grace you have been saved, through faith—and this not from yourselves, it is the gift of God—not by works, so that no one can boast. (Ephesians 2:8–9)

Salvation is the greatest miracle; therefore, accepting Jesus Christ as your Lord and personal Savior activates a personal relationship required to start your walk with Christ and live a life in the Spirit. This relationship, which is destined to lead toward figuring out and seeking your divine assignment on earth, will ultimately lead you to the divine anointing required to fulfill your destiny. Therefore, by accepting Jesus Christ as your Lord and personal Savior, you have received and accepted God's gift in John 3:16: "For God so loved the world that he gave his one and only Son, that whoever believes in him shall not perish but have eternal life." It qualifies you for a life in Christ and access to your gift of infertility. It is your responsibility to move beyond this level, and your path to promotion depends on your obedience to God.

Sin is a reproach that will rob you of this gift. In some cases, God will use you anyway, but you will bear the consequences of sin. You can neither be effective nor receive your gift of infertility until you forsake all and follow Jesus Christ. What you have received will be in constant battle with the devil, self, and worldly desires, but you must be determined to keep growing in the Lord and attain a life of holiness. To be successful at this stage, you must constantly and diligently seek God in prayer and Bible study. Your promotion is in your hands through the grace of God and the power of the Holy Spirit.

To achieve your destiny, the reason why you exist, the reason for the infertility in your life today, you must come to a point where you declare to yourself, like Joshua, "Choose thee this day whom you'll serve. As for me and my household, we'll serve the Lord." (Joshua 24:15)

CHAPTER 10

Seeking Your Gift

The Lord said to Abram after Lot had parted from him, "Lift up your eyes from where you are and look north and south, east and west. All the land that you see I will give to you and your offspring forever." (Genesis 13:14–15)

Everything you need to seek and operate in your gift is in the Bible. If you are serious about achieving your divine assignment and receiving your gift of infertility, you must study and meditate on the Word of God regularly. In prayer, God will talk to you Himself, set up divine helpers, and sustain you through trials and tribulation until you arrive at your destination and receive your gift. The gift is the sum total of the process, place, and price you paid to achieve your destiny. God delights in faithfully walking us through the process required to achieve His divine assignments, but we must trust Him and have faith that He who has begun a good work in us will complete it (Philippians 1:6).

Abraham's faith in God was counted as righteousness for him. He had to be separated from Lot in order for Abraham to move forward. Separation from close relationships is never easy no matter the circumstance, but he had to pay the price in order to achieve his divine assignment. That was one of the processes required to activate his gift, seek God, and enter into a quiet place free of quarrels and baggage from the past. Having paid the price and gone through the process, the size of his birthing place unfolded before his eyes. His spiritual eyes were opened to see the length and breath of his position and the inheritance that God had for him and his descendants. Remember that he was still Abram at this time, which meant he was yet to come into his actual position and attain his gift of infertility. Saul encountered Jesus Christ in Damascus and his life changed. He was isolated for only three days, but the journey and difficulties he encountered throughout his ministry were part of the process and price. Against all odds, and sometimes faced with grave threats to his life, he moved from one place to another in order to seek and operate in his gift.

How would you know if your assignment was destined to be local, national, regional, international, or global? It depends on your ability to identify where your gift will be manifested. These Four Ps (Prayer, Process, Place, and Price) cannot be established without the help of the Holy Spirit. To seek and identify your gift, here are some helpful steps. However, you must study the Bible and receive revelations for yourself. Rhema is a personal experience.

1. Quiet time with your Maker

> When the Lord brings you into the land of the Canaanites, Hittites, Amorites, Hivites and Jebusites—the land he swore to your forefathers to give you, a land flowing with milk and honey—you are to observe this ceremony in this month. (Exodus 13:5)

Seek the Lord in prayer. Do a spiritual retreat, and ask God for confirmation on the next move you intend to make. Ask Him regularly to show you if you are still in the right place. Study the Word of God, and identify scriptures that will encourage you and sustain you through trying periods. You will find that these scriptures will lift your soul when you are down and become the sword of your spirit. When these trials and temptations affect your body, the Word of God will restore your health and strengthen you. The only way to acquire this power and authority in Christ is to sincerely spend time praying and studying the Bible. Be focused, and always remember to ask for forgiveness for all your sins before you enter God's presence. Those who worship God must worship Him in spirit and in truth. Live a life of holiness and righteousness so nothing pollutes your fellowship with God. In this place of worship, He will draw near to you as you draw near to Him. He will reveal everything to you, and you'll have no doubt about your next steps. But you must remain disciplined and stay close to God. Most times, God reveals things to us in stages. You may need to go through a learning experience and develop spiritually to handle the next divine task or challenge that will enable you to receive His next instruction. Be vigilant and wise because the enemy will play many tricks to deceive and distract you. Also, you must discern God's instructions through spiritual authority He has placed above you. In 1 Samuel 3, Eli the priest guided Samuel toward hearing the voice of God.

2. Take that step

> At that time Mary *got ready and hurried* to a town in the
> hill country of Judea. (Luke 1:39, emphasis added)

Once you have prayed and received confirmation, start planning your journey—exit or trip. Don't waste time at all. Delay in this case could be a denial on your part. In order to move forward, certain people must exit your life. In the parable of the weeds (Matthew 13:24-30), the owner of the field encouraged his servants to leave the weeds and the wheat to grow side by side until the harvest. You may need to accommodate some personalities on your way to greatness, but don't mortgage your future to please people during your harvest season. You must first burn the weeds then gather the good seed in your field. People seek their salvation in many ways, and some rebellious ones will want to take down as many people as possible through undue influences and distractions. Be vigilant, for the adversary roams around like a lion seeking whom to devour (1 Peter 5:8). According to Matthew 5:29–30, let go of whatever will make you sin and deprive you of achieving your destiny. Be radical in defending your faith, salvation, and divine destiny. "His disciples remembered that it is written: "Zeal for your house will consume me." (John 2:17). It should be all about God and none of you. Nothing in this world matters more than your divine assignment, for as confirmed in Ecclesiastes 12:8, "Meaningless! Meaningless!" says the Teacher. "Everything is meaningless!'.

If the divine instruction is to stay or wait, don't allow any contrary direction to derail you. Waiting could be your test. Perhaps your divine assignment requires a great deal of patience and perseverance. Waiting could also mean that God is putting finishing touches on the resources that will aid your divine assignment. Waiting could also be the process of refining your character, habits, and values for your destination. Jesus Christ waited awhile before His divine ministry was activated. Moses spent forty years in the palace and forty years in the desert to understand the nature and circumstances required to lead the people of Israel out of Egypt. Waiting is good for you. God's gift is too precious to be rushed.

Perhaps if King Saul had waited for Samuel to offer the sacrifice, he would not have lost all and be rejected by God. If you receive a divine instruction to wait, make sure you remain faithful and diligent in the current place while God prepares you for your manifestation. Disobeying this instruction can cost you any second chances you may have at reactivating a divine destiny. Despite Shimei's rebellion against David, Solomon gave him a second chance and instructed him in 1 Kings 2:36–37, "Build yourself a house in Jerusalem and live there, but do not go anywhere else. The day you leave and cross the Kidron Valley, you can be sure you will die; your blood will be on your own head." But Shimei disobeyed and lost everything, including his life.

3. Life in the Spirit

> Blessed are those who wash their robes, that they may have
> the right to the tree of life and may go through the gates
> into the city. (Revelation 22:14–15)

"The fear of the Lord is the beginning of wisdom, and knowledge of the Holy One is understanding" (Proverbs 9:10). Wherever you find yourself, you must maintain a life of holiness and righteousness. The Bible tells us in multiple verses that our Heavenly Father is holy. Holiness is living to please God. Let your lifestyle within and outside your home please your Maker. Forsake all sins, be sanctified, and allow the Holy Spirit to work through you and conform you to the image of Christ (Romans 8:2). Be conscious of your sinful actions and desires (1 Thessalonians 4:3–7). Living a life of holiness and righteousness is a must for you to access your gift successfully.

Righteousness refers to being in right standing with God, which means living in faith. The size of your assignment will place a demand on your faith through the waiting and trial period, the storms, and ultimately receiving the gift. The larger and more significant your assignment, the more demand will be placed on your faith. Without faith it is impossible to please God. Abraham trusted God wholly and fully. Esther said, "If I perish, let me perish." (Esther 4:16). Your assurance should always be that God would complete what He has started in your life (Philippians 1:6).

4. Humility

> No one who lives in Him keeps on sinning. No one who continues to sin has either seen Him or known Him. (1 John 3:6)

When you arrive at this place of your birthing process, you must strip yourself of rank, reputation, and all earthly desires that could limit you like the rich man who went to hell and Nicodemus who sought Jesus at night. Our Lord Jesus left His heavenly place to come to earth. He subjected Himself to being placed in a womb, delivered in a manger, and traveling throughout His earthly ministry by foot and sea. He had the power to appear wherever He wanted to go; we saw evidence of that after His resurrection. But He chose to walk the streets, interact with the poor, share with people of all types, debate with His creation, and be humiliated by mere mortals. If Jesus Christ our Lord could do this, why do you need a grand entrance, a red-carpet reception, and a five-star package to commence and enter your divine assignment? Why are you setting terms and conditions before accepting your divine assignment and gift? Why are you looking down on people who may have been placed there as divine connections and destiny helpers? Why are you putting material possessions and worldly demands ahead of your divine assignment, ministry, and destiny? You need to check yourself. You may just be the architect of your current dissatisfaction with life. Seek God (Matthew 6:33).

Nonetheless, God may reward your faithfulness and longsuffering by ushering you into your destiny in grand style. God can honor you in any way He chooses for His glory. But you must remain humble to operate in your gift. Always remember where you started, where God took you from, and where you are going. The gift is yet to bless humanity, so do not get carried away with your entrance. Always return all the glory to God!

5. Total Surrender

> But the widow who lives for pleasure is dead even while she lives. (1 Timothy 5:6)

You cannot serve two masters, and you cannot mix two different things. When you step into this place, you must let go of all others and focus on God. Accepting your assignment will definitely cost you. Your ministry will place a demand on everything familiar to you. You must discern in prayer what you must let go in order to fulfill your assignment. Note that this must be in line with God's will; therefore, divorcing your spouse or abandoning your children is not God's will. Do not make decisions that are not backed up in the Bible. Abraham moved with both his immediate and extended family, but when it was time to let go of his extended family, they parted ways and he blessed them and never stopped praying for them. Similarly, Joseph did not divorce Mary to fulfill his assignment but sought God and received divine instructions to assist him in achieving his destiny and receiving the gift of infertility he felt when he first realized his new wife was already pregnant. Usually what you have to let go are relationships, habits, activities, and possessions that pollute or contaminate access to your divine assignment. Seek the Lord in prayer, and as you live a life of holiness and righteousness, these will be revealed to you. This demand may not be placed on you at inception, but before the fulfillment of the assignment, God will reveal it to you. Abraham started the journey with Lot (Genesis 12:4) but let him go as they went along when Lot's baggage became a distraction (Gen. 13:5–12). Out of the millions of people who left Egypt with Moses, only two—Joshua and Caleb—made it to the Promised Land. Be conscious of the fact that if you don't do it, God could raise some else. Also, cherish your waiting your period. Moses was in the wilderness for forty years, and Jesus served His parents quietly until when his earthly ministry began.

6. Create a Memorial

> Then the Lord said to Moses, "Why are you crying out to
> me? Tell the Israelites to move on." (Exodus 14:15 NKJV)

In a place your assignment takes you to, make sure you create a legacy whenever you encounter God. Abraham and his generation always built altars for the Lord at every place they went. In your place of work, become a star at work, add value to the company, and create something new. In business and other endeavors, do something that will impact humanity and improve the GDP of your country. "For many are invited, but few are chosen." (Matthew 22:14). Chosen ones do not take from the system; they recreate and leave a legacy. They fulfill their divine mandate for existence as detailed in Genesis 1:28. Do not be shortsighted. Do it quickly and move on to the next task required to complete your divine assignment on earth.

Sharing your testimony at the altar with sincere believers will encourage those still on their journey and give God all the glory for His faithfulness. That altar is your place of worship, which places a demand on the Lord to bless and empower you for the next level toward fulfilling your divine calling or ministry. Your divine assignment creates a legacy and blesses generations.

CHAPTER 11

Test for Your Gift

Who is it that overcomes the world? Only he who believes
that Jesus is the Son of God. (1 John 5:5)

The first sign that you have entered the journey that will lead to your divine assignment is conflict, battle, and warfare. All of a sudden, it looks like everything has turned upside down and against you. The battle intensifies, often taking new shapes and sizes. You begin to lose your peace and composure, including relationships, money, or health. The climax is an event that completely breaks you and challenges everything you've ever believed in. It could be the loss of a job, the death of a loved one, a failed project, a canceled contract, severe illness, or a major disappointment. While this event is devastating, it is usually the beginning of your victory and the discovery of your divine assignment.

Destruction or disappointment is a sign of a new beginning. It is a sign that either you have entered your calling or you need to be further processed before you can pursue your divine assignment. Oftentimes, when you recover from the devastation, you could find yourself right back to the point where the struggle began, but usually with a different perspective and a better understanding of your purpose. The second phase mirrors the point where the struggle started devoid of all former anxieties and depression. You work on your divine assignment, equipped with revelations and divine connections and with purpose and maturity.

The Dilemma Question

> Be wise in the way you act toward outsiders; make the
> most of every opportunity. Let your conversation be
> always full of grace, seasoned with salt, so that you may
> know how to answer everyone. (Colossians 4:5–6)

A dilemma offers choices and forces you to make active decisions that
significantly impact your present or future. Decisions are mostly activated
in the mind through one of the other senses, e.g., speech, sight, etc. Some
of your greatest battles while on your journey to receiving your gift of
infertility will be in the mind. The mind will deliberate the messages you
receive from God, challenge your convictions, make suggestions, argue
for or against your decisions, and attempt to influence your decisions.
Whenever you find yourself struggling to make a decision, stop and return
to God immediately. This is a dangerous zone to be in, and only the Holy
Spirit can direct you. You must stop and seek God immediately.

> For though we live in the world, we do not wage war as
> the world does. For the weapons we fight with are not
> the weapons of the world. On the contrary, they have
> divine power to demolish strongholds. We demolish
> arguments and every pretension that sets itself up against
> the knowledge of God, and we take captive every thought
> to make it obedient to Christ. (2 Corinthians 10:3–5)

Three examples of the dilemma question will give you perspective
on what to watch for. Eve's fall in the garden of Eden started with a
dilemma question in Genesis 3:1. Engaging in the conversation slowly
took her power and victory and robbed her of her divine destiny. The more
you engage in conversations that challenge your convictions and divine
instructions, the more you are drawn into submission and your worldly
eyes engage other senses to derail you completely.

A dilemma question can arise out of your disobedience and complete
consumption of what you think is your right. This self-consumption makes
it impossible to discern and obey the voice of God or promptings from
the Holy Spirit because your mind is focused on your own convictions. In

Genesis 4:6–7, God posed questions that could have stopped Cain from committing murder and losing his spiritual inheritance in God's kingdom. God rejected the offering but not Cain himself. If Cain had put self aside and heeded God's voice, he would have received the gift of infertility relating to the work of his hands. Cain's struggle with his convictions led him to murder his brother, Abel, even when God had cautioned him about what was going on in his mind.

A dilemma question can also arise when you engage in acts of deception, thinking you are smarter than everyone else and sneaking around in unbelief. In Acts 5:1–10, Ananias and Sapphira decided to deceive the apostles. Their premeditated acts of deception were challenged by Peter through many questions that revealed their sin. They died instantly because they lost the opportunity to repent and redeem their gifts of infertility in character. We always have warning signals when a dilemma question comes up, but our ability to discern this dangerous and overpowering spirit will not always depend on our level of spiritual maturity or standing before God. It is very tempting to apply human wisdom or seek advice from others at times like this, but only the Holy Spirit can help. Do not mortgage your gift on the altar of a dilemma question. Be careful how you seek and enjoy details, discussions, and debates, for they can distract you from your divine assignment.

In contrast to the above examples, John the Baptist in John 3:23–30 responded positively to a conversation that could have drawn him into a dilemma. When John was told that Jesus was drawing a crowd and baptizing on the other side of the river, he left no room for further analysis, interpretations, or gossip. He immediately reminded them of two points. First, "A man can receive only what is given him from heaven." In other words, Jesus was focusing on His divine calling while John was functioning in his. Therefore, "Mind your business." Secondly, he reminded them of his earlier prophesies about the coming of the Messiah and ended by saying, "That joy is mine, and it is now complete. He must become greater, I must become less" (vv. 29–30). This shows a man who understood that his divine assignment had been fulfilled and his gift of infertility delivered.

If John was not a man led by the Spirit of God, he would have engaged in unnecessary conversations, generated animosity, caused a scandal, became jealous, and stirred up strife in the land. This would have completely stolen his gift of infertility, killed his ministry, and destroyed the hope of generations. In Luke 23:39–43, one of the criminals crucified on the cross next to Jesus Christ asked Him, "Aren't you the Christ? Save yourself and us!" The other criminal immediately challenged him, saying, "Don't you fear God?" and used that opportunity to secure his place in paradise. If you are spiritually sound or strong enough, use the opportunity to share a message of salvation and love. To be successful at this, you must look to Jesus and seek guidance from the Holy Spirit through righteous living, prayer, and consistently renewing your mind and believing the Word of God. Your words have the power to build you or destroy you. Be guided by 1 Peter 3:15: "Always be prepared to give an answer to everyone who asks you to give the reason for the hope that you have."

CHAPTER 12

Despising Your Gift

O Lord, the hope of Israel, all who forsake you will be put
to shame. Those who turn away from you will be written
in the dust because they have forsaken the Lord, the spring
of living water. (Jeremiah 17:13)

Stop despising your gift! Sin, iniquity, idolatry, and acts of rebellion will
continue to create multiple layers of infertility in your life and deny
you of your divine access to your creator. Be sure not to be spiritually
dead or weak, asleep or ignorant. Ignorance is not an excuse. You must
be knowledgeable about the things of God. That's why God said in the
Bible, "my people are destroyed from lack of knowledge." (Hosea 4:6). You
can't be a soldier and go to sleep. Sleeping on duty is very dangerous and
leaves you vulnerable to the attacks of the evil one. You must guard and be
vigilant of your spiritual life, constantly being watchful in prayer, feeding
your spirit on the bread and water of life. A life devoid of the constant
presence of the Holy Spirit will suffer many challenges even if you think
you are obeying all the commandments. You must spare your five senses
of ungodly activities and associations capable of contaminating your body,
soul, spirit, and mind. How will you account for all God invested in you?
In the parable of the talents, the one who lost everything actually thought
he was being wise.

Live a life of holiness and righteousness. Jealousy, competition, strife,
rebellion, and sabotage will rob you of your blessing. If it is in a work

environment, office politics will take you nowhere as a child of God. Do not compromise your integrity, for promotion comes from God (Psalm 75:6–7). If it is in business or public service, corruption and malpractice will only destroy your assignment and future. Some people would argue that after all David, Paul, Moses, and Jonah were still used by God. God is merciful, but you present these arguments at your own peril. Stop pushing your luck. Remember, these powerful servants and men of God were processed and sanctified, but there were consequences for their actions. Paul did not see Jesus in the flesh, but he wrote most of the books in the New Testament. Moses did not go into the Promised Land, but he was present at the transfiguration. Jonah lived in the belly of a fish for three days, but he was given a second chance twice—first to complete his mission and second to have a conversation with God about his feelings. They all achieved their divine assignments and received their gifts.

Twelve Deadly Ds That Can Rob You of Your Gift

These are clear signs of spiritual blindness and can ultimately destroy you if you do not desist from that life right now.

1. Debasement

Therefore, I urge you, brothers, in view of God's mercy, to offer your bodies as living sacrifices, holy and pleasing to God—this is your spiritual act of worship. (Romans 12:1)

Debasement can eliminate you and your gift completely. It takes control of your body, soul, and spirit. This means devaluing that which belongs to God by offering it up for sin or idolatry. In Revelation 2:14, 20 is specific reference to sexual immorality and eating food sacrificed to idols. Why then should you offer yours to ungodliness even after you have heard the Word of God and probably confessed Jesus Christ as your Lord and personal Savior? Romans 1:18–27 clearly says how severe these ungodly acts are regarded by God.

The wrath of God is being revealed from heaven against all the godlessness and wickedness of men who suppress

the truth by their wickedness, since what may be known
about God is plain to them, because God has made it
plain to them. (vv. 18–19)

The Bible clearly tells us in our opening text that your body is the
temple of the Holy Ghost. Fornication and adultery are forbidden and will
rob you of your divine destiny. This includes breaking faith with a marriage
covenant (Malachi 2:11–16), being unequally yoked, divorce, and abuse.
If the One who created you despises these things, why do you engage in
them? Flee from sin and allow God to use your life to His glory and honor.

You have to stop engaging in detestable pagan practices that entangle
you in sin and bondage. Allowing your kindred or family traditions to
supersede your faith is very dangerous. You cannot serve two masters. God
is holy, and "God is spirit, and his worshipers must worship in spirit and
in truth." (John 4:24). Some of these evil practices tied to your ancestral
beliefs will bind your generation to covenants untold and indescribable.
These could also be by your associations and activities in foreign nations
(2 Chronicles 33:2). In Daniel 3, the people were made to bow down and
worship the king and idols. But Daniel refused and the Lord delivered
him from all his trials and promoted him. God clearly tells us in His ten
commandments not to have any god besides Him. All acts of debasement
have severe consequences and will definitely keep the Spirit of the living
God away from you; so far from you that you'll never live to fulfill your
destiny. Onan spilled his semen on the ground to keep from producing
offspring for his brother (from fulfilling his duty as a brother-in-law), but
what he did was wicked in the Lord's sight, so he put him to death (Genesis
38:9–10).

Repent and ask for forgiveness. It's a stubborn stronghold, so you will
need help to overcome. Seek spiritual counsel from a Holy Spirit-filled
church. Beyond prayer and counseling, you'll need to be in constant
fellowship with other believers and the church. The process of renewing
yourself will be facilitated if you have access to sound teachings about
God's love for you, Jesus Christ's sacrifice on the cross for you, and the
Holy Spirit's nearness to you. You are not alone, but you've to be an active
participant in your deliverance process. For additional guidance, read 1
Timothy 4; Acts 15:29; 1 Corinthians 8; and 1 Corinthians 10.

2. Depraved Mind

> Furthermore, since they did not think it worthwhile to retain the knowledge of God, he gave them over to a depraved mind, to do what ought not to be done. (Romans 1:28)

The things listed in further verses of this text are everyday acts people take for granted, evil done as part of one's habit or character. The danger is that it becomes enthroned in your mind, entrenched in your rules of engagement, and enlivened in your standard of living. It starts to feel right, gives you audacity to encourage others involved in these acts, and liberty to engage in them on a continuous basis. This begins a path of self-destruction where you may lose complete control of your sense of direction and ultimately your gift of infertility. It starts with access to your senses—the things you see, hear, and meditate upon. Be very careful what goes through your five senses of sight (eyes), hearing (ears), speech (mouth), feeling (heart or mind), and smell (nose). These are vulnerable access to your spiritual life and easily targeted by ungodly influences. Guard these senses with your life. Don't watch, listen, or think about things that you know can never please God. The appeal through sight, heart, or mind is extremely dangerous and overwhelming. Your thoughts should be in line with Philippians 4:8. Otherwise you will pollute, contaminate, and corrupt your body, soul, and spirit, which affect your worship and fellowship with God. Don't rely on your willpower to overcome temptations, "For our struggles is not against flesh and blood, but against the rulers, against the authorities, against the powers of this dark world and against the spiritual forces of evil in the heavenly realms." (Ephesians 6:12).

Your mind is the battlefield. You have to exchange the conversations and imaginations in your heart for the knowledge of God. Only the Word of God can help you. The solution is stated in Psalm 1:1–3:

> Blessed is the man who does not walk in the counsel of the wicked or stand in the way of sinners or sit in the seat of mockers. But his delight is in the law of the LORD, and on his law he meditates day and night. He is like a tree planted by streams of water, which yields its fruit in

season and whose leaf does not wither. Whatever he does prospers.

Also, study the scripture for specific strongholds according to the area that you struggle most with as a Christian. Do self-examination and seek the presence of God. Greed (Proverbs 15:27), pride (Proverbs 21:4), covetousness, bribery (Proverbs 17:23), and corruption are all evidence of debasement in your life. You cannot ignore these things and forsake your divine assignment. Psalm 107:17–18 clearly states, "Some became fools through their rebellious ways and suffered affliction because of their iniquities. They loathed all food and drew near the gates of death." These are acts of rebellion that will rob your gift of infertility, so you must flee now, for the end is destruction. God is merciful, and His thoughts for us are good. Your state of infertility may have been as a result of one or more of these sins listed in the opening text, but God's grace is sufficient for you.

3. Disobedience

Raise the war cry, you nations, and be shattered! Listen, all you distant lands. Prepare for battle, and be shattered! Prepare for battle, and be shattered! (Isaiah 8:9)

All through this book, the consequences of disobedience have been greatly emphasized because it would cost you and your generation more than the temporary pleasure you derive. A divine mandate was issued to man at creation, wrapped in love but despised through disobedience to God's instruction in the garden of Eden. Your actions can destroy the destiny of many people and cause them to lose their gifts. A nation consists of people with different divine assignments. You could be the divine connection and access to their fulfilling their own divine assignment and coming out of infertility. Any failure on your part is utter disobedience and wickedness. Spiritual blindness and rebellion made the children of Israel complain so much that Moses got angry and stuck the rock twice in complete disobedience to God's instruction. It cost Moses entering the Promised Land. He saw it but could not enter it. Disobedience will make you lose courage and open a door for fear into your life. Out of that generation of Israelites, only Joshua and Caleb made it to the Promised

Land because they gave a good report and did not create fear among the people like the other ten spies.

Disobedience in giving can cause delay or hinder your ability to access your gift of infertility. You might need a seed to trigger that harvest. Obedience is critical at this point, and delayed obedience can delay the manifestation of your divine assignment. However, you must live a life of holiness and righteous for your offering to be accepted by God. Giving money obtained in sin cannot give God glory. You are only wasting your time, especially if you are showing off for men to see you. Receiving accolades from men cannot aid your access to your gift of infertility. The process of development along your growth path could also trigger challenges that could be mistaken for a life of infertility created by sin and disobedience. But always remember, if you are living a righteous life, God will walk with you and you will come out victorious.

4. Disquieted Spirit

Why are you downcast, O my soul? Why so disturbed within me? Put your hope in God, for I will yet praise him, my Saviour and my God. (Psalm 43:5)

This is a silent killer. It means for your soul to be continually anxious, uneasy, restless, and dissatisfied. It robs you of a life of holiness and righteousness because you are always internally focused, seeking things to satisfy yet find pleasure in none. The absence of the Holy Spirit in one's life is the beginning of this affliction. Little wonder why David cried out in Psalm 51:10–12,

Create in me a pure heart, O God, and renew a steadfast spirit within me. Do not cast me from your presence or take your Holy Spirit from me. Restore to me the joy of salvation and grant me a willing spirit, to sustain me.

Without the Holy Spirit, we are finished. In 1 Samuel 16:14, the spirit of the Lord departed from Saul and an evil spirit from the Lord troubled him. Note that in the previous verse, David had already been anointed to take Saul's place as king. A disquieted spirit alters your countenance and leads to rebellion. It triggers acts of jealousy (Esau), thoughts of murder (Cain), anger (Moses), ego, and disobedience (Saul). This makes you vulnerable to your enemies like Samuel, causes you to lie like Ananias, or become judgmental like one of the women who came to King Solomon with a dead son. These will alienate you from the fellowship of believers until it isolates you enough to rob you of your purpose. In extreme cases, it could cause depression, madness, and ultimately kill you. It's a silent killer because it takes you unaware, starts as murmuring and complaining about your circumstances, and, if unchecked, graduates into severe affliction and conditions. It usually manifests when you are about to enter your destiny. Only the entrance of the Word of God can save you because it brings light and dispels darkness. Good and evil may look the same in this condition, but you must urgently run to seek deliverance from a Holy Spirit-filled church. Also, clothe yourself in praise, offering praise to God and ordering your conversations according to Philippians 4:8–9:

> Finally, brothers, whatever is true, whatever is noble, whatever is right, whatever is pure, whatever is lovely, whatever is admirable—if anything is excellent or praiseworthy—think about such things. Whatever you have learned or received or heard from me, or seen in me—put it into practice. And the God of peace will be with you.

5. Discord

> These six things the LORD hates, Yes, seven are an abomination to Him: A proud look, A lying tongue, Hands that shed innocent blood, A heart that devises wicked plans, Feet that are swift in running to evil, A false witness who speaks lies, *And one who sows discord among brethren.* (Proverbs 6:16–19 NKJV, emphasis added)

Stirring up suspicion, gossip, and false witness detests God. Our opening test clearly states this is as an abomination before God. You might feel justified and sure of what you are saying from a human perspective, but you have been called to live above the devices of the evil one and the allure of the flesh. Often people engage in this sort of behavior to show off access to perhaps privileged information or nearness to authority. It could simply be mischief and envy. There is no excuse; it is simply evil and will rob you of your gift of infertility and divine destiny. Stop it now! Confess this weakness to God and ask for mercy and the grace to overcome. Include Psalm 51 and Philippians 4:8–9 as part of your hourly or daily prayers, and dispense this darkness in your heart through constant study of the Word and fellowship with the brethren. Engaging in this behavior even in your heart will manifest in the physical because the Bible mentioned in Matthew 12:34, "You brood of vipers, how can you who are evil say anything good? For out of the overflow of the heart the mouth speaks." Verse 14 of our opening text describes the wicked thus: "Perversity is in his heart, he devises evil continually, he sows discord." Do not mortgage your divine assignment so cheaply, for you are only robbing yourself.

6. Doctrines

> Do not be carried away by all kinds of strange teachings.
> It is good for our hearts to be strengthened by grace, not
> by ceremonial foods, which are of no value to those who
> eat them. (Hebrews 13:9)

"Then you will know the truth, and the truth will set you free." (John 8:32). Seeking knowledge and direction outside the Bible is only contaminating your body, soul, and spirit. Those other doctrines will only derail you for as long as you want to remain in darkness. Ignorance is not an excuse. God created us and graciously gave us the Bible to guide us into all truth. Yet we seem to have time for everything else but the one thing we need to be whole and achieve our destiny. Stop this deception in your life. "Seek first the kingdom of God and His righteousness and all other things shall be added unto you" (Matthew 6:33). All those false religions and teachings cannot help you. "A man who strays from the path of understanding comes to rest in the company of the dead" (Proverbs 21:16). The level of your divine assignment demands that you seek only the things of God and allow the Holy Spirit to guide you into all truth. Get into fellowship with believers, and plant yourself in a Holy Spirit-filled church. Allow the servant of God who has been placed in your life to mentor you, and stop running from one place to another seeking doctrines that are of no value to your life. This will only delay or deny your gift of infertility.

7. Deception

> This is what the Lord says: "Cursed is the one who trusts in man, who depends on flesh for his strength and whose heart turns away from the Lord. He will be like a bush in the wastelands; he will not see prosperity when it comes. He will dwell in the parched places of the desert, in a salt land where no one lives." (Jeremiah 17:5–6)

People engage in acts of deception in order to please men and find favor. In Genesis, deception led to the fall of man and God sent Adam and Eve out of the garden of Eden. Deception denied Samson of his vision and ultimately a life. From the moment he was deceived, he lived a life of misery, hardship, and pain. Acts of deception, cheating, denial, and doubt are all evidence of deception in your life. Proverbs 20:23 says, "The Lord detests differing weights, and dishonest scales do not please him." How can you obtain your gift of infertility when you continually engage in this evil behavior? You might think that no one can see you, but God sees everything. You are only robbing yourself of your divine destiny. These evil practices will keep you in a constant state of infertility. Even if you successfully deceive people and get away with it, this will only be a temporary victory of your debased self. You are robbing yourself of much more than you will gain. Men might even celebrate your achievements, but deep down, you'll never know peace. "What good is it for a man to gain the whole world, yet forfeit his soul? Or what can a man give in exchange for his soul" (Mark 8:36-37). Flee from these things so you can receive your gift of infertility and achieve eternal life.

8. Disclosure (Nondisclosure)

> God is a righteous judge, a God who expresses his wrath every day. (Psalm 7:11)

You must confess your sins and ask for God's forgiveness. Hiding unconfessed sin in your heart will only rob of you of your gift of infertility. What have you done that is so grave you cannot humble yourself and cry to God for forgiveness? God is a righteous judge. Nothing takes Him unaware. He knew you did those things, and yet He allowed His only beloved Son to die for your sins. The price is already paid, so all you have to do is to appreciate the sacrifice Jesus Christ made on the cross. Stop living in guilt and regret and hiding from your Creator. David committed adultery, Rahab was a prostitute, Moses committed murder, Jacob deceived people, Jonah was stubborn, Mary Magdalene was possessed by demons, and Paul persecuted Christians. But look how God used them to advance the kingdom of heaven. This shows that you still qualify to be used mightily by God no matter how dark you've lived. You will only perish if you go back to your vomit after God has delivered you (Proverbs 26:10). God is merciful, loves you dearly, and is waiting for you to receive your gift (Romans 11:28–32). You are a chosen vessel; that's why you feel that conviction of unconfessed or hidden sin. Pride and arrogance might be keeping you from humbling yourself at the foot of the cross, but you are only denying or delaying your gift before death snatches you from the earth and you will have lost everything anyway. Amos 8:11 says, "The days are coming," declares the Sovereign Lord, "when I will send a famine through the land—not a famine of food or a thirst for water, but a famine of hearing the words of the Lord."

9. Dishonor

> When Elizabeth heard Mary's greeting, the baby leaped in
> her womb, and Elizabeth was filled with the Holy Spirit.
> (Luke 1:41)

Dishonoring people, especially those placed in authority over you, is a guarantee for living a life of infertility and failing to receiving your gift. People are placed in authority over you for a reason, a season, and a purpose. In your birthing experience, your stages of development are determined by the interactions you have with these people. Usually, they are older than you, but in other cases, they are younger. Therefore, you must not despise anyone based on age, gender, nationality, or out of arrogance. You must seek to learn from and soak up all experiences. Spiritually discern why this person has been placed over you at this particular time or sent to guide you into your new level of assignment. Contact with a divine connection would make your gift leap with joy, a feeling unmistakable because it belongs to God. Every encounter creates testimony, praise, and worship, giving God all the glory and honor, such as "The Magnificat: Mary's Song of Praise" (Luke 1:46–55). Dishonor robs you of this divine privilege to celebrate your gift and destiny before God. The person who triggered my hunger for deep spiritual things was not only younger but also seemed beneath my status in every way. It took the Holy Spirit to help me recognize why she had been placed in my growth path at that time. Her childlike ways were often annoying, and I was sometimes very mean to her. But the more I ignored her, the more distant I became to my birthing process. Arrogance only hurts you and denies you of your gift and inheritance. You may think you have achieved all because of your worldly status, but be careful not to miss the real reason why God sent you to this earth.

10. Death

> I tell you the truth, whoever hears my word and believes him who sent me has eternal life and will not be condemned; he crossed over from death to life. (John 5:24)

Physical death marks an end only if you have not achieved your divine assignment. However, you may find yourself in a state of depression or spiritual death that limits your desire, ability, or capacity to take the steps required to liberate yourself and achieve your divine assignment. Even if you are stable in life, don't get too comfortable, and stop making excuses. Don't allow life to force you into a difficult situation before you humble yourself and seek God. Remember that Esther took a big risk in executing the task in the king's palace. She took a risk that could have robbed her of all the wealth, comfort, and glamour, but she chose to seek Jesus Christ through the help of the Holy Spirit. She focused on a spiritual exercise by embarking on a dry fast for three days with her co-laborers. She also humbly took the advice of her divine helper, her uncle Mordecai, who had helped her attain her position in the king's palace in the first place. Even when you ultimately attain first access and assignment, remain humble and submissive to your spiritual authority. The children of Israel escaped from Egypt, crossed the Red Sea, and fed on manna from heaven, yet it did not end their struggle and they remained spiritually blind. They still needed God and the guidance from their spiritual authority in Moses and later Joshua to develop, mature, and ultimately make it to the Promised Land and win battles against nations.

II. Double Mindedness

> But when he asks, he must believe and not doubt, because he who doubts is like a wave of the sea, blown and tossed by the wind. The man should not think he will receive anything from the LORD; he is double-minded, unstable in all he does. (James 1:6–8)

It is possible for you to miss a divine opportunity out of ignorance, doubt, suspicion, skepticism, carelessness, stubbornness, arrogance, pride, or lack of preparedness. Many people are struggling with infertility today simply because they missed a divine opportunity to learn and get promoted through the hierarchy. You spend time casting and binding your enemies when you should look inward. The only way to reverse this is by seeking God earnestly with all your heart. Leave no room for the enemy to sow seeds of doubt and contempt, causing you to worry and think of negative things. Don't allow yourself to be derailed. Stay focused, and defend your calling with your body, soul, and spirit. Jonah found himself in the belly of a fish before he repented and accepted an assignment God had given him. Moses's anger denied him physical access to the Promised Land he had so looked forward to. King Saul's temperament cost him the throne and his relationship with God. Samson's negligence, sexual immorality, and love for ungodliness robbed him of his life as he remained in prison until the last days of his life. If you feel too big to seek your Creator, who do you really worship? Your stubbornness could be the limitation. Some have completely ignored or despised their divine assignment because of social networks and media associations. The consequence is either delay in the manifestation of their gift or living a secret life of frustration and misery. Remember, it's "not by power, nor by might but by the spirit, says the Lord" (Zechariah 4:6). You are nothing without Jesus Christ.

12. Dining

> Food gained by fraud tastes sweet to a man, but he ends up with a mouth full of gravel. (Proverbs 20:17)

The provision and sharing of food is a place of testing that gives access to your mind. Your disposition is vulnerable to exploitation, enticement, distraction, and deception. Adam and Eve lost their place in the garden of Eden over receiving and sharing a fruit. Esau sold and despised his birthright over a meal (Genesis 25:29–34). Gifts and favors are bargained over and exchanged on the dining table for good or bad. Be careful of the interactions you engage in when you are hungry or sitting at the dining table with associations you entertain over a meal. Proverbs 23:1 says,

> When you sit to dine with a ruler, note well what is before you and put a knife to your throat if you are given to gluttony. Do not crave his delicacies for that food is deceptive.

And Romans 14:20 says, "Do not destroy the work of God for the sake of food. All food is clean, but it is wrong for a man to eat anything that causes someone else to stumble."

In Daniel 1:8, Daniel resolved not to defile himself with the food set at the king's table, and God blessed him with knowledge and understanding of all kinds of literature and learning. Daniel could understand visions and dreams of all kinds. He would have exchanged these gifts for pleasure if he had not exercised discretion and discipline by limiting his diet to vegetables. This also earned him gifts and honor before the king (Daniel 2:48). Ultimately, he survived the lion's den because of his steadfastness in serving the Lord (Daniel 6:21). In Genesis 30:14–16, Rachel and Leah's negotiation over mandrake plants led to the swapping of sleeping rights with their husband and ultimately an exchange of fertility for that season.

In Genesis 27:4–31, Jacob requested Esau to prepare food for him in exchange for his blessing. Over this same food preparation, Rebekah conspired with Jacob to deceive Isaac, and Jacob ultimately coveted his brother's blessings, which set off a war between them. In Genesis 47, people in Egypt and Canaan traded their wealth for food, which ultimately left them in the servitude of the pharaohs. In Exodus 16:3 and Numbers 11:4–5, the thought of food kept the children of Israel in bondage to Egypt even though they had physically left the land. This mind-set contributed to their long period of infertility—an eleven-day journey that took them forty years. In 1 Samuel 2:27–36, Eli's family lost their heritage because his sons ate the food offering meant for God. In 1 Kings 13:20–28, the man of God ate falsely and lost his life

Don't rob yourself of your gift of infertility. Our LORD was tempted in the wilderness with food, but "Jesus answered, "It is written: 'Man does not live on bread alone'." (Luke 4:4). Take your eyes off physical food and exercise discipline in your daily consumption of food and drink. Avoid all forms of illicit drinks and use food for the nourishment of your body, soul, and spirit in a manner that would not rob you but rather bless you. Jesus said unto them in John 4:34, "My food is to do the will of Him who sent me and to finish his work." In Joshua 5:9–12, manna seized the day the children of Israel ate the produce from the land as they were getting ready to possess their possession. In 1 Kings 17, the Zarephath woman gave Elijah food in exchange for abundance for the rest of her life. In Esther 7, Esther confronted Haman over a banquet in front of the king and won freedom for Jews in exchange for Haman's life. In 1 Samuel 9, Samuel invited Saul to the high place to eat with him, and he was subsequently anointed as king.

CHAPTER 13

Protect Your Gift

Forget the former things; do not dwell on the past. See, I am doing a new thing! Now it springs up; do you not perceive it? I am making a way in the desert and streams in the wasteland. (Isaiah 43:18–21)

"But do not forget this one thing, dear friends: With the Lord a day is like a thousand years, and a thousand years are like a day." (2 Peter 3:8). It is never too late to activate your divine assignment. You may have advanced in age like Abraham and Sarah, or been derailed by committing grievous sin like Moses, or living a life of shame like Rahab, or persecuted like Christ and Paul. But remember that God has the final say. "For my thoughts are not your thoughts, neither are your ways my ways," declares the LORD." (Isaiah 56:8) He also does not judge by appearance and remains faithful even when we are untruthful. Once you have decided to forsake your old ways, He will back you up. You may experience the consequences of your ungodly ways, but the burden will be lighter than if you had remained in a life of sin and iniquity.

Perhaps you simply gave up on your destiny and became weary. God is able to empower and energize you. Elijah begged God to kill him soon after he had accomplished a more divine task by calling down fire from heaven and killing all the prophets of Baal. He was exhausted and afraid of Jezebel's threat to deal with him. But God sustained him and sent a divine messenger to assist him and prepare Elijah for the next level of his divine assignment. God is able! Giving up is not an option for the gift that awaits you; therefore, arise for the time to favor you has come (Psalm 102:13). Wake up, take up your mantle, and follow Christ. Allow Him to redirect your steps and help you achieve your divine task. Abraham and Sarah waited twenty-five years to see Isaac, Moses lived in the desert for forty years, and the children of Israel took forty years to arrive in the Promised Land—a journey that should have taken eleven days. They were going round and round in circles as they were being purged and processed. Rahab recognized the divine opportunity to turn a new page. She took advantage of the situation and made an immediate change that impacted her destiny, family, and ultimately the children of Israel. Ruth remained focused and persevered even in the face of insecurity and uncertainty. She followed her mother-in-law, Naomi, to an unknown destination and remained committed until she met Boaz and her life changed. She was willing to try a new culture and a new trade and take risks in order to achieve her divine destiny. Naomi's other daughter-in-law, Orpah, took a different step, and we never heard the rest of her story. You must trust God even in the face of uncertainties, difficulties and unforeseen circumstances.

Through the Darkest Valley

> Even though I walk through the valley of the shadow of death, I will fear no evil, for you are with me; your rod and your staff, they comfort me. (Psalm 23:4)

Throughout your life and ministry, the enemy will deploy strategies to derail you at the edge of your breakthrough. These are temptation, persecution, and accusation, all of which can occur in unpredictable timeframes.

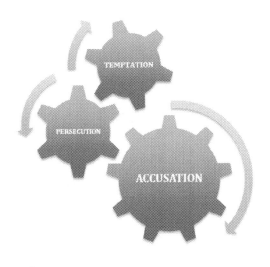

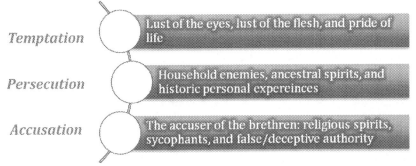

The symptoms and side effects of these would manifest as periodic cycles of affliction and seasons of infertility. However, you must remain faithful because failure will delay or deny your gift of infertility. These trials are tests of faith that will stretch your belief system. However, for some people it will manifest as an affliction, which could distract them from the real objective of what they are passing through. In all these things, God constantly assures that He will never leave you nor forsake you. It takes the mercy and grace of God, with the help of the Holy Spirit, for you to discern that it's all part of your journey and the source of your gift.

In a season of temptation, use the Word of God. In a season of persecution, depend on the Holy Spirit. In a season of accusation, exercise your spiritual authority and allow God to fight for you.

> The kings of the earth take their stand and the rulers gather together against the LORD and against his Anointed One. (Psalm 2:2)

Oftentimes, mature Christians and servants of God miss the mark at the state of accusation. Revelation 12:10–12 talks about the accuser of the brethren, but verse 11 says, "They overcame him by the blood of the Lamb and by the word of their testimony; they did not love their lives so much as to shrink from death." Jesus Christ's ultimate destination became our victory. In facing your accusations, remember the finished work on the cross that was demonstrated by the blood shed for your victory and the testimony it symbolizes. It's not about you, your credibility, or your life, so stop trying to defend yourself and focus on the good news of Christ. It's not the time to read your accolades, reiterate your conquests, and show off your achievements in life and ministry as proof of your innocence. Outward appearances are irrelevant (Galatians 6:12–13). This is a spiritual battle, and the weapons of warfare are not canal, so put on the armor of God and fight a good fight of faith. You are already redeemed, so enforce your victory by proclaiming the defeat on the cross and the power in the name of Jesus Christ and the Word of God. The more you seek justification from men, the more intertwined you become in the web of accusation being woven and orchestrated by the enemy of your soul. The architects of this crisis may be near or far, but the target is you, your ministry, or family, and ultimately your divine assignment. Oftentimes, the channel or vessel used to attack you is within or unexpected, so it will be very painful from a carnal perspective. But "be in the spirit," and don't get caught up in your emotions.

Finish Strong Like Jesus Christ

> The Spirit of the Lord is on me, because he has anointed me to preach good news to the poor. He has sent me to proclaim freedom for the prisoners and recovery of sight for the blind, to release the oppressed, to proclaim the year of the Lord's favor. (Isaiah 61:1–2)

This text was also quoted at the inception of Jesus's ministry in Luke 4:18–19. Throughout Christ's earthly ministry, and especially in the final days, he faced all three of these strategies and conquered. Therefore, you, too, will conquer. Despite all these attacks, you must remain focused and faithful. In facing His *temptations* (Luke 4:1–3), our Lord and Savior Jesus Christ always used the Word of God ("it is written") to silence the enemy. In *persecution* (throughout the Gospels), He responded with divine teaching, preaching, and instruction inspired by the Holy Spirit. His communion with the Father was often in silence at the quiet place of prayer, where He drew strength from above to persevere and fulfill His divine assignment. These spiritual exercises equipped Him for life on earth, and miracles, signs, and wonders characterized His earthly ministry. His acts and words were based on what He heard from the Father. During His trials, He remained focused, discerning the enemy's distractions, while listening for the voice of God in the Spirit, even leaving Him in a physical state of exhaustion and thirst as He walked to face death on the cross. The fourteen stations and seven words on the cross constitute a legacy undeniable even by the enemy himself. Jesus Christ appointed Saul (later called Paul) as His apostle in a time of persecution, who went on to write most of the books in the New Testament after a quiet season of three years incubated by the Holy Spirit. In *accusation* (Luke 23), Jesus maintained dignity molded in the fruits of the Holy Spirit despite the state of isolation and betrayal. He had been betrayed by an insider, Judas Iscariot; abandoned by his own disciples; arrested by a diverse crowd of chief priests, temple guards, and elders; and denied by His closest disciple, Peter, only to face three levels of accusation by people who were both near and far.

1. The Council of Religious Leaders, Elders, and People

> The fool says in his heart, "There is no God." They are corrupt, their deeds are vile; there is no one who does good. (Psalm 14:1)

These were people entrusted with enough knowledge to discern the presence of the Son of God, yet they missed Him and became instruments of the enemy. They would look for one close to you to use for their plan to destroy you. The council of religious leaders and elders paid one of the twelve disciples of Jesus Christ, Judas, to betray Him. In ministry, it could be incessant attacks from other men and women of God or your congregation. It could also be domestic problems with your spouse or co-laborer in Christ. In other cases, it might be false teachings and acts upheld by persons in positions of authority, such as bosses, parents, pastors, priests, or prophets you listen and submit to, which constantly puts you in a state of condemnation rather than create a genuine conviction that leads to repentance. In this state of accusation in Luke 22:66–71, Jesus Christ simply acknowledged that nothing He could say to them would make a difference, so he focused on proclaiming who He was as the "I AM," Son of God, and emphasized His position at the right hand of the Father. So when people accuse you, simply tell them who you are in Christ, a joint heir to Christ, seated at the right hand of God the Father. Don't be intimidated or deceived into entering unholy and unrighteous conversations, which can rob you of your gift of infertility.

2. Pontius Pilate: Political/Government Institutions

> For our struggle is not against flesh and blood, but against the rulers, against the authorities, against the powers of this dark world and against the spiritual forces of evil in the heavenly realms. Therefore, put on the full armor of God, so that when the day of evil comes, you may be able to stand your ground, and after you have done everything, to stand. (Ephesians 6:12–13)

This is the person in authority or people in leadership who have the power to stop the accusation or mediate in the crisis yet will not for fear of persecution. They extend the most comfort in times of crisis yet accept a hand of friendship with the enemy of your soul behind the scenes. These people avail themselves as access for evil. Pilate became friends with Herod (Luke 23:12) in order to either enforce justice or defend his position of authority. They are not loyal to anyone, including their family members. Pilate's wife tried to stop him, but that didn't help. He absolved himself of all responsibility as compromise. Some people call it being politically correct, but it's usually at the expense of another company enemy. John 18:28–37 reveals the motives and thrills of these sorts of leaders or persons in authority. Once again, Jesus Christ told him who He was but remained silent when he referred back to the accusation and false testimony of the first group, the council of religious leaders, elders, and people. He made a good confession (1 Timothy 6:13) and refused to be drawn into opposing ideas (1 Timothy 6:20–21). Always refuse to be drawn back into the battle you have won and silenced. The person you are talking to now may not find fault in what you have done or explained but will want to judge you by the testimony of the people. His or her credibility with you can be exploited to draw you back to a past event or state of accusation you have conquered. This is a direct challenge of your calling that could deceive you into entering unholy and unrighteous conversations in order to derail you and deny you of your gift of infertility. Be quick to rebuke it! We saw this several times in the life of Simon Peter. In Matthew 16:23, "Jesus *turned* and said to Peter, 'Get behind me, Satan! You are a stumbling block to me; you do not have in mind the things of God, but the things of men'" (emphasis added). Note that people's access to you makes it possible for them to confront you more than once, so be watchful. Jesus was sent back to Pilate a second time by the third accuser. Always pray for the family, friends, and workers closest to you not to be used as an agent of Satan. As Jesus told his disciple, "Simon, Simon, Satan has asked to sift you as wheat. But I have prayed for you, Simon, that your faith may not fail. And when you have turned back, strengthen your brothers." (Luke 22:31-32. You can admonish and pray for them, but don't send them away except they remain unrepentant. Focus on the word God has given you, no matter the circumstance, and remain in His presence until He establishes your victory.

3. Herod: Accuser of the Brethren

> Do not give dogs what is sacred; do not throw your pearls to pigs. If you do, they may trample them under their feet, and then turn and tear you to pieces. (Matthew 7:6)

This is the enemy who has been waiting for your downfall and possibly the architect of your current predicament. Herod had wanted to meet Jesus Christ for a long time. Luke 9:9 says, "But Herod said, 'I beheaded John. Who, then, is this I hear such things about?' And he tried to see him." On this day of trial, when Christ was brought before him in Luke 23, it simply gave Herod pleasure to see Jesus ridiculed and mocked. That day, he became friends with his enemy, Pilate, in order to execute a plan he had hatched for a long time. He simply extends his misery by petty mockery and cowardice. Here in this state of accusation, Jesus Christ did not respond at all. There was no basis for conversation because He knew that the matter was settled and victory was His. Our opening text warns us not to waste our sacred and valuable on pigs (Deuteronomy 14:8) and dogs (Revelation 22:15; Philippians 3:2).

In the Final Analysis

I have given you authority to trample on snakes and scorpions and to overcome all the power of the enemy; nothing will harm you. (Luke 10:19)

For a child of God on the path to fulfilling a divine assignment, this is a state of confidence and victory in God when you face the one who has been seeking to destroy you and find that he or she doesn't have the authority to execute his or her plan because all authority belongs to God. It could also be when your greatest fear in life happens to you. It's unsettling yet a sign of victory and expansion. That's why a small stone took down Goliath, a praise-filled shout brought down the walls of Jericho, a blind Samson pulled down the temple, killing more enemies, and bars of iron were put asunder in a heavily guarded prison. Believe in Jesus Christ, for the Bible tells us in 1 Timothy 6:12, "Fight the good fight of the faith. Take hold of the eternal life to which you were called when you made your good confession in the presence of many witnesses." In verses 13–16 of the same text, we are reminded of His good confession in front of Pontius Pilate and the undeniable supremacy of God. From here onward, you are unstoppable, so you must lift your head high and pursue your divine assignment in order to receive your gift of infertility and achieve eternal life with Jesus Christ. Finally, our Lord and Savior, Jesus Christ, reassures

Nnenna Okoro

us again in Revelation 1:18: "I am the Living One; I was dead, and behold I am alive for ever and ever! And I hold the keys of death and Hades."

Following are the key highlights to note as you study this chapter:

- Identify your enemy, but trust God completely.
- Be strong and very courageous
- Be prepared and disciplined
- Obey instructions and execute them excellently.

CHAPTER 14

Conquering Infertility in Life

"For I know the plans I have for you," declares the LORD, "plans to prosper you and not to harm you, plans to give you hope and a future." (Jeremiah 29:11)

The suffering during a time of infertility can cause you to question life and faith. It could be so bad that you may not know where to turn or what to do to lift the pain. The beauty for some people, especially true Christians, is that they know who will win in the end. However, for others, it is difficult to see where help will come from. Jesus Christ is the answer to everything, but you must play your part to live and enjoy the gift of your current infertility. God is faithful, and His thoughts for us are good. If we can give good gifts to fellow men and women, God is committed to doing even better for us. God always rewards those who diligently seek Him. However, we must show our interest and a strong desire for our gift of infertility. The nearest place to start is by encountering Him in an intimate relationship with the help of the Holy Spirit and your diligence through studying the Bible. This brings you into divine fellowship with the Holy Trinity and expounds your promises. It gives you keys to unlock your destiny and access to testimonies of those who have successfully received their gifts of infertility. Stop shortchanging yourself; rise up to take your rightful place in Christ. Why beat around the bush to find a treasure when you can appropriate your rights as a joint heir with Christ? In addition to seeking God diligently, you must live a life of holiness and righteousness and include different types of spiritual exercises, such as praying, fasting, and giving as part of your lifestyle. Full details of these concepts have been explained in earlier chapters of this book.

Here are a few helpful tips on coping with infertility and living victoriously in the face of these challenges.

Spiritual Life

You have said, "It is futile to serve God. What did we gain by carrying out his requirements and going about like mourners before the Lord Almighty?" (Malachi 3:14–15)

Check yourself! No one can mock God. If you are pretending to be a Christian and still living a life that is unworthy, unholy, and unrighteous, your spiritual life will remain bankrupt and infertile. You can't serve two masters (James 3:11).

Motives, Hidden Secrets, and Sin

Many are the woes of the wicked, but the LORD's unfailing love surrounds the man who trusts in him. (Psalm 32:10)

What are your secret motives for attending church and participating in religious activities? How serious is your fellowship with your brethren and God? What do you do when no one is watching? What do you watch on TV? What sites do you visit on the Internet? Are you still holding onto your old lifestyle and habits? Flee from the appearance of sin. Are you still living your old life, engaging in the same habits that put you in bondage and visiting the same friends? Don't assume that you can change people overnight because you are now born again. The danger of accommodating their excesses will soon draw you back into a life of sin. "Submit yourselves, then, to God. Resist the devil, and he will flee from you'. (James 4:7). "Do not be yoked together with unbelievers. For what do righteousness and wickedness have in common? Or what fellowship can light have with darkness?" (2 Corinthians 6:14). Stop justifying your associations by misunderstanding and misrepresenting the Bible. You need to be spiritually grounded to take on certain battles in life. Putting on the whole armor of God requires varying degrees of spiritual growth to prepare you to resist the flesh, the world, and the devil. Close all doors to the enemy and open yourself to the Holy Spirit. "Do not conform any longer to the pattern of this world, but be transformed by the renewing of your mind. Then you will be able to test and approve what God's will is – his good, pleasing and perfect will." (Romans 12:2).

Lack of Discipline

> Produce fruit in keeping with repentance. (Matthew 3:8)

Being a Christian does not exempt you from being a disciplined member of your society or family. If anything else, your standards and ethics should be worthy of emulation by others. Don't stand there preaching to everyone else and quoting the Bible when your character and values are nothing to write home about. Close your mouth and fix your life. Humble yourself and pay attention to the obvious weaknesses in your life. Don't flaunt your titles in church to impress and deceive the world into thinking you are a person of integrity. Pay your taxes, obey government rules, show love to your neighbor, be diligent at work, adhere to the teachings of Jesus Christ, and obey the commandments in the Bible. For the gifts and calling of God are without repentance (Romans 11:29).

Spend Quality Time with God

> But I trust in your unfailing love; my heart rejoices in your salvation. (Psalm 13:5)

God loves worship. HIS desire is for us to draw near to HIM and HE will draw near to us. To access higher realms of your gift and anointing, you must spend personal, intimate time with God on a regular basis. Participating in different church activities simply keeps you busy and in fellowship with other Christians, but it is not sufficient to tap that anointing needed to release your gift. The threshing floor is critical to your obtaining your promise and embracing your gift. God desires to reveal Himself to us with the help of the Holy Spirit. It's our responsibility to seek Him with all our hearts and minds, and then He will reveal great and mighty things to us. He will also warn us of imminent danger and attacks.

Desire to be Used by God

> Then I would still have this consolation—my joy in unrelenting pain—that I had not denied the words of the Holy One. (Job 6:10)

You were born for a purpose. God wonderfully made you for a reason. Don't live your life on your own terms. Desire to be used by God. "Seek ye first the kingdom of God and His righteousness and all other things shall be added unto you" (Matthew 6:33). Don't postpone your salvation and spiritual growth because of worldly pleasures and material possessions. Procrastination is dangerous because you do not know what will happen in the next moment. At the end of the day, you will give account of your stewardship on earth. Seek a life in the Spirit and the gifts of the Holy Spirit. Don't be afraid. If you are confused about the events in the Acts of the Apostles, seek to understand and not castigate those using theirs or pretend that these gifts do not exist. God gave us those gifts for a reason. At these end times, God is seeking for his children. Your comfort zone can become a hindrance to the manifestation of your gift. This comfort zone includes both your physical location and spiritual beliefs. Step out in faith, and join the real army of God!

Career, Labor, and Investments

> The Lord will open the heavens, the storehouse of his bounty, to send rain on your land in season and to bless all the *work of your hands*. You will lend to many nations but will borrow from none. (Deuteronomy 28:12, emphasis added)

Acknowledge That You Need Help

> I will instruct you and teach you in the way you should
> go; I will counsel you and watch over you. (Psalm 32:8)

Owing to past successes and sometimes ego, people don't seek help when things start going wrong in their jobs, ministries, and businesses. As soon as you notice a demotion, lack of promotion/increase, or declining profits, act fast and seek God in prayer. Don't spend time talking to everyone else except God, who is the Alpha and Omega, the Beginning and the End. You may have taken a wrong step and simply need a new direction. You may be hindering yourself by your choices and decisions. Your inner man may be resisting your increase and promotion to the next level. In that case, all you need is mentoring and coaching. At other times, it's just the beginning of a new experience or season in your life in which you have to discern, so don't despise the birthing process. However, if it's an attack from the enemy, the sooner you take authority as God's child and recover what is being stolen from you, the better for you. "The thief comes only to steal and kill and destroy; I have come that they may have life, and have it to the full." (John 10:10). There's no need pretending to family and friends that all is well when you can hardly sleep at night. You may need to engage in prayer and fasting to fight this battle. "No, in all these things we are more than conquerors through him who loved us." (Romans 8:37). Always remember, you are more than a conqueror through Christ who strengthens you.

Revisit Your Passion

> Do not work for food that spoils, but for food that endures
> to eternal life, which the Son of Man will give you. On
> him God the Father has placed his seal of approval. (John
> 6:27)

It's never too late. Time is on your side. Moses was called at age eighty. Sarah and Elizabeth received their gifts in old age. Age is not a barrier in the kingdom of God. Only the world dictates age limits, such as retirement age, maximum fertility age, and others. Methuselah made it to the Book of Records because he attained a ripe old age. Studies have confirmed that longevity has reappeared to humanity, and all the renewed emphasis on the environment is evidence of a call to return to basics. So make a fresh start, and stop struggling for crumbs off the tables of people living in their destinies. People think that having worldly connections and mindlessly expanding their network makes them important. But you are only valuable to people when you are operating in your gift; otherwise, you will be one more contact to delete when they change their phone. Seek divine connections and destiny helpers.

Some people are currently experiencing infertility because they are spending time in a profession to impress their family and friends. This includes parents who disregard their children's gift and derail them by insisting on particular courses of study and profession. Parental guidance is important, and obviously a child should be forced out of illegal activities by all means. However, a responsible child made to struggle through life because of the path he or she has been forced to follow is counterproductive. He or she tries to do different things, are not focused on anything, and never succeed. This leads to infertility of his or her labor. If you notice, such children become frustrated, do not perform with a spirit of excellence, and cannot be promoted beyond a certain level. Ultimately, some derail completely and become a menace to the society. Others act out their frustration in other ways, such as abuse, irresponsible lifestyles, and lack of interest in the things of God. Some even blame God for their situation. In this cases, bless these children and help them to revisit their passion. Support them morally and financially. If you are an adult, seek spiritual counseling from an anointed pastor or priest and lead that child back to Jesus Christ. The Holy Spirit will take over and transform your life.

Retrain Yourself

> A whip for the horse, a halter for the donkey, and a rod
> for the backs of fools! (Proverbs 26:3)

Go back to school if you have to acquire new skills or update your knowledge. Tell yourself the truth. What do you need to become a better person, worker, student, professional, or businessman or woman? Apply your faith, and seek that next level, even if you don't have money. If it's a trade you want to learn, submit yourself for training, and be humble. Ruth found her gift while gleaning behind reapers in the field and ended up in the genealogy of Jesus Christ. Joshua was under Moses's stewardship and earned the right to lead the children of Israel into the Promised Land. Elisha abandoned his profession and got a double portion of Elijah's anointing. Peter, a fisherman, followed Jesus Christ and became an apostle who did mighty exploits for Christ. He is also referred to as the Rock and was the first pope of the Catholic Church. Leave your rank, family background, previous titles, and work experience at the door and take up the challenge.

Pay Your Tithes and Offerings

> "Bring the whole tithe into the storehouse, that there may be food in my house. Test me in this," says the Lord Almighty, "and see if I will not throw open the flood-gates of heaven and pour out so much blessing that you will not have room enough for it. I will prevent the pests from devouring your crops, and the vines in your fields will not cast their fruit," says the Lord Almighty. "Then all the nations will call you blessed, for yours will be a delightful land," says the Lord Almighty. (Malachi 3:10)

This is extremely important. Many people take the subject of paying tithes and offerings for granted even though the Bible clearly states the benefits and negative consequences of this divine act established by God Himself. You can't rob God and expect to bear fruit. A tithe is 10 percent of ALL your income and nothing less. The size of the giving shouldn't bother you if you truly believe that God blesses people. Stop justifying yourself with worldly wisdom, and release God's share of the income so you can obtain the promise He already attached to tithing in the Bible. "God is not a man, that He should lie, nor a son of man, that he should change his mind. Does he speak and then not act? Does he promise and not fulfill?" (Numbers 23:19). If He said it, He will do it. How dare you rob God and expect to receive your gift! If it is not preached in your church or emphasized by your priest or pastor, read the Bible for yourself. You don't wait for anyone to feed you physically, so why wait to be fed spiritually? Learn to feed yourself spiritually by studying the Bible. Understand the differences and principles between tithes and offerings (including periodic church offerings, seed sowing, first-fruits, prophetic giving, etc.). If you believe you are already in the prophetic process for your gift, make sure you pay your tithes and offerings. Ecclesiastes 11:2 says that giving protects your future from disaster, and you must give according to the method and manner that God has commanded. Using your discretion to give alms/charity here and there, or sponsoring projects or making donations, is not paying your tithe. Where you pay your tithe also matters, so be strategic about how you invest your money in the kingdom of God. Plan your giving in advance. It's not an out-of-pocket decision you make while you are in church. Prepare your financial seed from home, and pray over it, according your needs, and claim the promises in the Bible. The ground where you sow your financial fruit is very important. Don't be emotional or sentimental. It could impact your increase and promotion.

Choose Your Mentor Wisely

> I am the vine; you are the branches. If a man remains in me and I in him, he will bear much fruit; apart from me you can do nothing. (John 15:5)

Most people give advice based on their perspective on life, which may be very different from what God has planned for you. The Bible clearly tells us that the only way to access God is through His beloved Son, Jesus Christ. Similarly, according to our opening text, the key to fulfilling your divine assignment is directly related to how you remain in Christ. Remaining in Christ gives you access to the spiritual nutrients required to be successful as a "branch of the vine." Your only source for accessing the gifts and fruits of the Holy Spirit is linked to the vine. Who do you listen to? What qualifies this person to be your mentor? Has the person any experience in what you are passing through or where you are going? It is important that you guard your gift by choosing mentors and counselors who will nurture the dream and not derail you. Other times, you may require wise counsel to launch you into your destiny. Seniority, bloodline, wealth, education, admiration, and political and religious affiliation should not influence your choice of a mentor. Simply allow the Holy Spirit to guide you. Always check his or her counsel against the Word of God. Anything that is contrary to a life of holiness and righteousness can never be the will of God for your life.

Explore Alternative Investment Opportunities

> Can both fresh water and salt water flow from the same spring? My brothers, can a fig tree bear olives, or a grapevine bear figs? Neither can a salt spring produce fresh water. (James 3:11–12)

If you are experiencing infertility in your investments, explore other sources. Perhaps your gift is targeted at the wrong resources or being processed through a channel that isn't right for your seed. Have you the required knowledge, expertise, or advice for what you are doing? "My people perish for lack of knowledge" (Hosea 4:6). Oranges can never grow on apple trees. Fish only thrive in water. Some crops will never grow in tropical regions. Similarly, check your finance and investment advisers. Are you leaving your investment in able hands? Have you trusted people who are gifted in that area of business? Have you hired skilled staff and people of integrity to manage your investments? Is the entire value chain of your business legal? You can't claim to be doing legitimate business if you are aware that a link in the value chain is corrupt. It may work for a while, but the day of reckoning shall surely come. Ignorance is not an excuse because you are should have done your due diligence. Seek God's guidance so you don't waste your gift.

Body and Soul

> "But for you who revere my name, the sun of righteousness will rise with healing in its wings. And you will go out and leap like calves released from the stall. Then you will trample down the wicked; they will be ashes under the

soles of your feet on the day when I do these things," says the Lord Almighty. (Malachi 4:2–3)

Healing Starts in Your Mind and Heart

Your healing comes from only one source: Jesus Christ, our Lord. The main effect of sickness is that it robs us of peace of mind and health in body. "But he was pierced for our transgressions, he was crushed for our iniquities; the punishment that brought us peace was upon him, and by his wounds we are healed" (Isaiah 53:5). Therefore, you must constantly reject anything contrary to the promise of God. The battlefield is in your mind. You must cast down everything that exalts itself above the Word of God. If you still think sick in your mind and heart, your body will not respond to the healing process. You must take hold of the promises of God concerning healing and continuously proclaim them, tap into them, and possess them in your soul. Reading and studying the Bible constantly with tenacity is the medicine you need. You might be taking medication for a condition that only requires a word from God.

Forget the Pity Party

Out of the same mouth come praise and cursing. My brothers, this should not be. (James 3:10)

You are only hurting yourself if you constantly rehearse your symptoms and feel good about letting everyone know how they have to help you because you are sick. You should be speaking the promises of God, not celebrating your suffering. Your words are powerful, and these contradictions are not helping you. Quit the pity party, and stop those making those phone calls, seeking the next person to listen to your cries. The pain and discomfort can be overwhelming, and sharing with a trusted person can alleviate the suffering, but the end result of that conversation should be prayer and Bible study. Ultimately, God is the healer. Even when you attend miracle services, your faith will activate the healing in your body. Spend time in God's Word, building your faith, and in the company of fellow believers, who can help your faith. Anyone around you who inspires the pity party or stirs up negative feelings about your condition should be avoided like the plague. They are sowing seeds of discord in your mind, which is evil. If they delight in such conversations, let them keep it within their own environment and not contaminate yours. You have to be decisive about your destiny.

Exercise Your Faith

> To this John replied, "A man can receive only what is given him from heaven." (John 3:27)

As you begin to appropriate God's promises, your mind and heart start to heal and your body begins to respond. Some people will receive instant healing while others will go through a process. In faith, start doing things you couldn't do before. Once you feel like taking on a new challenge, say a prayer, believe God, and just do it. Do not be afraid. In the case of the woman with the issue of blood in Matthew 9:20–22, her total healing and wholeness happened as she took a step of faith and touched Jesus Christ's cloak. "Jesus turned and saw her. "Take heart, daughter," he said, "your faith has healed you." And the woman was healed from that moment." (Matthew 9:22)

Seek Spiritual Help

> In fact, no one can enter a strong man's house and carry off his possessions unless he first ties up the strong man. Then he can rob his house. (Mark 3:27)

Evil is at the heart of most illnesses. If your sickness is persistent or seems to be a generational issue, you must seek spiritual help. You may need to go through deliverance, which is a period of prayer and fasting. During this process, you will learn to use the appropriate word of God for your specific circumstances and exonerate yourself from the effects and consequences of ancestral curses and pagan worship that may exist in your family lineage. Most people have received healing simply by denouncing these linkages to ancestral spirits. Make sure you seek help from a place of worship that is Spirit-filled and recognizes deliverance as a right of every child of God. Be careful not to engage in deliverance that focuses only on binding the enemy without reminding you that God has given you the authority over all the powers of the enemy (Luke 10:19). Such places will only instill fearfulness and not faith, leaving you vulnerable to further attacks of the enemy without the corresponding armor to fight back. "For God did not give us a spirit of timidity, but a spirit of power, of love, and self-discipline." (2 Timothy 1:7).

Take on Your Spiritual Authority in Jesus Christ

> But he was pierced for our transgressions, he was crushed for our iniquities; the punishment that brought us peace was upon him, and by his wounds we are healed. (Isaiah 53:5)

Revelation 12:11 says that they overcame by the blood of the Lamb and the word of their testimony. The blood of Jesus has everything required for your healing. You must stand on that and proclaim it over every condition. Take Holy Communion as often as possible, and constantly claim your healing by the blood of Jesus. At the mention of the name of Jesus Christ every knee must bow; therefore, you have to speak to that situation always in the name of Jesus Christ. Neither grow weary nor discouraged, for your healing is taking place already. Also, use this spiritual authority to help those who are sick. Some healings have taken place when people exercised their spiritual authority in praying for others with similar conditions. In all things, you are more than a conqueror.

Marriage

> For this reason a man will leave his father and mother and be united to his wife, and the two will become one flesh. This is a profound mystery—but I am taking about Christ and the church. However, each one of you also must love his wife as he loves himself, and the wife must respect her husband. (Ephesians 5:31–33)

If you are experiencing unhappiness and despair in your marriage, return to God. He ordained marriage in the beginning. The Holy Spirit should guide your decisions and actions. If you do this, not only will God give you wisdom and strength, but the purpose for the experience will also be revealed to you. Your destiny is closely tied to whatever you are going through right now. "Seek ye first the kingdom of God and His righteousness, and all these other things will be added unto you" (Matthew 6:33). Your victory resides in you.

Stay under the Living Water

> Jesus answered her, "If you knew the gift of God and who it is that asks you for a drink, you would have asked him and he would have given you living water." (John 4:10)

John 4 lets us into a divine conversation and shows that openness to Christ can end a state of infertility. In verse 15, the real reason for the woman's antagonism and desire to have the living water was revealed. In this statement, we can see that a singular factor has been responsible for resentment and instability in her life—a feeling of lack of appreciation can become a seed into many issues in marriage. Oftentimes, people cover up the main issue and manifest their anger and frustration by exaggerating nonissues into major family crises. Hidden anger and resentment are dangerous seeds that lead to manipulation, depression, and other extreme behavior that the enemy would use to destroy you and your gifts. Don't hide the truth from Jesus Christ. If you can't talk to anybody else, go to your knees into your prayer closet or a desert place and cry out to Jesus. Remember, our Lord intervenes in many ways. He could send someone to minister to you, reveal something for you to read, remind of a story to instruct you, give you wisdom and/or inspiration. You must bring your soul and spirit back to the truth for you to move forward. As a married person, your spouse should be next in line for this conversation. It's no surprise that in the next verse, Jesus asks the woman about her husband. In this case, she probably thought that changing the men in her life would bring the joy she was seeking. But true joy and happiness can only be found in Christ. The Holy Spirit has to dwell in you before you can move forward. There's no situation that God cannot handle, for He controls the heart of men.

Talk to Your Spouse Sincerely

> To the married I give this command (not I, but the
> Lord): A wife must not separate from her husband …
> And a husband must not divorce his wife. (1 Corinthians
> 7:10–11)

Oftentimes, we want to run away from the very person God has placed in our lives to be our covering. Before you were born, God saw today and the circumstances in which you find yourself. Attempt to approach your spouse with a sincere heart and keep the conversation focused on the main issue on your mind. Talk to him or her with humility, respect, and a positive attitude. Esther prepared herself with praying and fasting before she approached her husband with her case. Her case involved revealing her identity and demanding something that was contrary to the information his trusted lieutenant had told him, yet her approach gave her favor before God and man. Abraham revealed his feelings of fear and inadequacy to Sarah in order to solicit her support to cover for him. Ruth cleaned herself up before she entered the presence of Boaz. Hannah's husband showed compassion for her pain and struggle by showering her with gifts. Rebekah could only play the deceitful game she did with Jacob because she understood how to enter the presence of her husband and get his attention. You have been placed in your spouse's life to help him/her succeed, understand you, raise the next generation, and achieve his/her destiny. Your success as a husband or wife is critical to receiving your gift of infertility. Don't play games with your spouse, especially in times of crisis. Don't take your spouse for granted. Be sincere, supportive, loving, and truthful. At the end of the day, there lies your true identity. Where you think you have lost the credibility to communicate effectively and be trusted, spend some time on yourself to work on this weakness. Train yourself to become believable and trustworthy again and resolve to be consistent and supportive. Within this waiting period, trust God to see you through. Stay in the presence of the Holy Spirit and accept this season for what it is—a waiting period. Be the best husband or wife you can be with the help of the Holy Spirit. Your spouse will surely notice and come to you even before you reach out.

Be Careful What You Hear

> Who will bring any charge against those whom God has
> chosen? It is God who justifies. (Romans 8:33)

As a married person, you should be extremely careful about your associations, conversations, and friendships. The enemy will always seek ways to create confusion in a marriage and oftentimes will use people around you. Little comments, remarks, and insinuations could magnify and create lifetime issues. Stop gossiping, complaining, and murmuring. These are grave sins against your marriage, husband, and God. People listening to you do not necessarily have your interest at heart. You have become a source of entertainment for them. How can you expect a turnaround in your situation when you've opened it up for public debate and analysis? You may be forced to seek counsel from a godly person, but be sure that you have been led to speak to this person by the Holy Spirit. Due to frustrations, you may have spread the news about the issues you have for anyone who cared to listen. But today is a new day, so stop and focus on God. He alone can help you. Stop listening to people who only seek your hurt and rejoice over your pain. They have no respect for you and cannot help your situation. Don't be deceived by the closeness of the person, friend, or relation you are confiding in and sharing your woes. Only God can help you! Household wickedness could be the source of your problems. Be careful! Even when you hear about other people's experiences, resolve in your heart that your case is different. All things work together for good to them that love God (Romans 8:28). Bad counsel can rob you of your anointing and gift.

Marriage Is Supernatural

> Who has done this and carried it through, calling forth
> the generations from the beginning? I, the Lord—with
> the first of them and with the last—I am He. (Isaiah 41:4)

Being truly married in the eyes of God brings you into the realm of the supernatural. Marriage was part of God's creation, entrusted with creative abilities and endowed with partnership likened to how Jesus Christ, God

Himself, feels about the church. It is a ministry that must not be toiled in the flesh. It is spiritual, and every aspect of it should give God all the glory and honor. Examine yourself today, and ask yourself if you have truly accorded your marriage the reverence it deserves. Have you served your spouse in a manner that gives God all the glory and honor? Have you loved your family like Christ loves His church? Do you treat this sacred entity God that has entrusted you with levity or grace? Are you experiencing infertility in your marriage because you have reduced its worth and are probably feeding the family with crumbs? Crumbs here mean the least you can offer of yourself and your abilities, resources, and love. Where have you missed it? Return to God, and watch how He gives beauty for ashes. Divorce should not be an option in the body of Christ. Before you tow that path, study your Bible thoroughly on the subject, take into consideration all the conditions tied to your decision, and seek God first without a heart of pain. Allow the Holy Spirit to minister to you.

You Are Precious beyond Description

> The Lord is the strength of his people, a fortress of salvation
> for his anointed one. (Psalm 28:8)

Difficulties can make you feel worthless. The words you hear every day from family members, especially your spouse, can be oppressive and even send you into a depressive state. You were beautifully and wonderfully made. These are mere mortals with carnal minds and unstable in all their ways. God cares and loves you more than you can ever imagine. Before you were born, He knew you. He formed you in your mother's womb and endowed you with precious gifts. No matter the circumstance you find yourself in today, God's love hasn't changed. He is watching over you, and you truly deserve the best. If you find that the source of infertility in your marriage resides in something you cannot explain, perhaps you are seeking a gift buried inside of yourself. You may have neglected an assignment because of the obligations of marriage and business of life. The restlessness within you could be a need to fulfill your calling. Simply drawing closer to God, participating in godly activities, deepening your relationship with the Holy Spirit, or opening yourself to study the Bible at the foot of Christ can uncover the need that set off this feeling of infertility. Go into a fasting and prayer season, and trust God to reveal the source of this inadequacy to you. God is faithful, and creation is earnestly waiting for the manifestation of sons and daughters of God. You are one of them, so step up and take your place in destiny before it is too late.

Womb

> Sing, O barren woman, you who never bore a child; burst into song, shout for joy, you who were never in labour, because more are the children of the desolate woman than of her who has a husband. (Isaiah 54:1)

Guard Your Spiritual Life

This is the classic definition of infertility and often affects women. It is a great source of heartache and depression for a family. This makes you vulnerable to fake intercessors and ministries. You become defenseless to family and friends who either want to refer you for additional spiritual counseling or give your details to all sorts of people claiming to be praying for you. Also, the prayer for the fruit of the womb is one of the most popular in most churches, a constant reminder of your situation. While the right church or ministry projects faith and gives you hope, other foolish people label you. This pressure forces you to seek help from all sorts of places and people. Be careful! No one can pray your prayer for you. Don't create new and additional issues in the foundation of your fruit and corrupt your gift. Trust God and no one else. Even when you have to pray with someone, never forget that God's eyes are on you. Learn to discern the spiritual background of the person seeking to help you. God said, "Worship the LORD your God, and his blessing will be on your food and water. I will take away sickness from among you, and none will miscarry or be barren in your land. I will give you a full life span." (Exodus 23: 25-26). Therefore, trust GOD completely and your gift will surely manifest.

Invest in Your Relationship with Your Spouse

> Husbands, in the same way be considerate as you live with
> your wives, and treat them with respect as the weaker
> partner and as heirs with you of the gracious gift of life, so
> that nothing will hinder your prayers. (1 Peter 3:7)

Anyone who gets into marriage strictly for procreation will surely be destabilized if they find themselves still seeking the fruit of the womb after a few weeks, months, and years of marriage. The companionship should be given priority in order to solidify the foundation of your marriage. Most marriages collapse even after they have children. The pressure of raising kids and managing other aspects of life can be overwhelming. Enjoy your marriage and plan your future while you wait for your kids to come. Don't allow outsiders, pain, and the grief of disappointing news from the doctors contaminate your relationship with your husband. Give him time, and do special things together. Talk to him, but if you feel that a particular subject is a trigger for your troubles, agree to a strategy for dealing with it. Be supportive of each other's careers and social life. Don't create suspicion, avenues for distrust, or open the door for marriage interference. Flee from the appearance of evil. Be protective of each other and constantly reaffirm your love for each other. In cases where your family members have become a nightmare, take it to God. Hannah did just that in 1 Samuel and God heard her. Perhaps you've been enduring that for a long time, but focus and let not God's presence depart from you. Your struggle is part of the process. Infertility of the womb is extremely difficult, sometimes unbearable, especially when everyone around you seems to be getting pregnant with ease. But nothing you do can change the situation. But God can. Seek Him, for He is a faithful God. He will not be one second late when your time to receive your gift comes.

Get Busy, Have a Vision

> Therefore, my brothers, you whom I love and long for, my
> joy and crown, that is how you stand firm in the Lord,
> dear friends! (Philippians 4:1)

An idle man or woman is the devil's workshop. Make sure you occupy your time with a career, business, ministry, volunteer work, or anything else that keeps you busy *except sin*. Don't just sit at home for extended periods of time because you are hoping a child will show up. Women have had their babies at times of war, and some have lost their babies even while on complete bed rest. God is in control of everything, so trust Him completely. Staying idle and focusing on how to conceive and have a baby has worked for some women, but the consequence is usually lack of self-fulfillment, frustration, and health issues. If you must stay at home, keep your mind active by studying always and attending good religious, professional, and social activities.

Prepare for Your Child

> And Adam was not the one deceived; it was the woman who was deceived and became a sinner. But women will be saved through childbearing—if they continue in faith, love and holiness with propriety. (1 Timothy 2:14–15)

This is an act of faith. It could be in terms of preparing a baby room by faith, buying baby items, learning from a friend on maternity leave, spending time with other people's children, or looking after your body in preparation for conception and motherhood. "Looking after" includes losing weight, eating right, and maintaining a healthy lifestyle. Some people are sensitive about letting other women touch their babies/children, so be careful when offering to help so you don't hurt your relationship with your friend. Don't take it personally! Whatever you choose, do it by faith. Name your children, and put up a cheerful countenance always. Cry when you are overwhelmed, but don't camp there.

If you lose a pregnancy or a child during this time, seek God, mourn the loss, and move on. Seeking God is very important because you could receive divine healing and instructions that will help you. Get medical help to ensure your body is ready for your next baby. Don't give up! Don't carry your bitterness and presumptions into your next pregnancy. Remember Jabez in the Bible! Allow each child to start with a new slate, and don't corrupt your child's destiny with your fear and emotional state. Your gift may be residing in your child, and the size of your assignment determines the length of time that you wait. Letting go could also speed up the arrival of your gift. You are being processed to nurture a child destined to impact his generation. Never become bitter or jealous to avoid contaminating your seed. Also, remember that many women have had multiple births after the loss of a baby or pregnancy. So trust God!

Attend religious services by anointed men and women of God. Observe spiritual exercises at your local parish or church. Miracles do happen at such Holy Spirit-filled environments. Sometimes you need God's servant or messenger to speak your gift into existence and encourage you. In the Bible, Sarah, Hannah, and Elizabeth had similar experiences. Draw strength from the fact that they all had their babies and received their gifts of infertility.

There is a final word for these special couples in the next chapter of this book.

Family

> Then the Lord said to Moses, "I will rain down bread from heaven for you. The people are to go out each day and gather enough for that day. In this way I will test them and see whether they will follow my instructions." (Exodus 16:4)

Lack of proper foundation in things of God and absence of the Holy Spirit triggers infertility in a family. Such families are devoid of love, loyalty, peace, and kindness, so they cannot be fruitful. They despise themselves more than their enemies outside the home and breed enmity, criminality, and disgrace. Other times, it could be exposure to the negative influences of friends and society, knowingly and unknowingly.

Identify the Source of the Dysfunction

> One God and Father of all, who is over all and through all and in all. (Ephesians 4:6)

A dysfunctional family life usually starts with sin and lack of discipline on the part of parents, children, or significant members of the extended family. In Genesis, Rebekah encouraged Jacob to deceive his father, Israel, which created long-standing conflict with Jacob's twin brother, Esau, and entrenched deception in Jacob's character. Some members of the family thrive by sowing discord and creating internal camps. Oftentimes, this leaves everyone exhausted, suspicious, and resentful. The first step is to identify the source of the problem. You might be unable to tackle this head-on, so you will need the help of a true man of God to counsel you on the best approach. Ask yourself deep questions about the foundation of your family. Could this be in the bloodline? Was it the result of sin or an external influence allowed into your home? Are you the problem? What triggers these incidents? How can you mend the broken pieces? God controls the heart of men, so you must seek God and ask for a revelation. Once you are convinced about the course of action to take, prayerfully commit everything to God in prayer and take the next step. You might just be the one God will use to turn things around.

Instill a Solid Spiritual Foundation in Jesus Christ

> Therefore put on the full armor of God, so that when the day of evil comes, you may be able to stand your ground, and after you have done everything, to stand. (Ephesians 6:13)

The Bible is filled with teachings about how we should conduct ourselves as individuals and family members. It guides us on our divine roles and responsibilities as children and parents. Start early to develop your children's interest in God and spiritual activities. Enable them to flow in their divine calling by exposing them to the right fellowship and environment. Hannah handed Samuel over to God, allowing Samuel to stay with Eli to nurture the call upon his life and the promise she had made to God. The only way to fix a dysfunctional family is to return to God. Bring fellowship, prayer, and Bible study back into the home. Ensure that all family members attend church services and identify with the things of God. Recognizing that each person has been called and chosen by God for divine tasks gives us the responsibility to support one another throughout this journey. Pray for one another, and let all your conversations give glory and honor to God. Love everyone, show empathy, and carry one another's burdens. Where there is the absence of a parent for positive or negative reasons, fill that gap and do not let members of your family disintegrate for whatever reason. If this has already happened, seek God now and ask for grace to fix the situation through the help of the Holy Spirit.

Destroy Foreign Objects in Your Home

> Do not be anxious about anything, but in everything, by prayer and petition, with thanksgiving, present your requests to God. (Philippians 4:6)

The entrance of foreign objects into a home can trigger strife within a family. A home once at peace suddenly becomes dysfunctional because their environment has been invaded by evil. These objects could either be gifts, souvenirs, or a person. It could also be objects deliberately planted by a member of the family who has joined ungodly associations. This could be out of ignorance of the real impact of his or her association with this new society. If you suddenly find strange things happening in your home, seek counsel and spiritual help. Don't be afraid, for fear will worsen the situation. Fear will make you depend on your strength and create unnecessary scenes to the pleasure and entertainment of the evil one. Take everything to God in prayer. He sees everything and will open your spiritual eyes to see the source of this sudden disruption in your family. It could even be ancient covenants made by your ancestors being renewed through ignorant acts and practices. It takes only one person to create untold havoc to a people. The children of Israel lost the battle at Ai because one person defiled the camp by taking objects against God's counsel. You might need to anoint your house. At this point, exercising your spiritual authority in Jesus Christ becomes extremely critical to avoid losing your home and the spiritual inheritance of your generation. Be discreet about discussing this with people who can't help you. Remain focused and disciplined throughout this season.

Nation

For to us a child is born, to us a son is given, and the
government will be on his shoulders. And he will be called
Wonderful Counselor, Mighty God, Everlasting Father,
Prince of Peace. (Isaiah 9:6)

Today's leadership is selfish andlacks spiritual depth. You may think
there is very little you can contribute to your nation's state of infertility, but
the righteous should pray. "For the eyes of the Lord are on the righteous
and his ears are attentive to their prayer, but the face of the Lord is against
those who do evil." (1 Peter 3:12). We are called to influence nations, and
your gift of infertility must go beyond your environment to bear fruit.
The wealth of every nation includes both its natural resources and people
especially the righteous.

Pray for Good Leadership

Righteousness exalts a nation, but sin is a disgrace to any
people. (Proverbs 14:34)

Gone are the days when kings are led by personal dreams and
visions revealed to them by God. With Joseph and Daniel, their gift of
interpretation of dreams for men in authority gave them access to leadership
and enabled them to achieve their gift of infertility. However, both of them
lived a disciplined life of holiness and righteousness in order to attain
their exalted positions. Continuously pray to God to give your country a
leader chosen by God, like He chose Moses and Jacob to lead the nation of
Israel our of bondage through many battles and into the Promised Land.
God also advised Moses on the seventy elders chosen to assist him. It is a
first step, and as many more righteous ones join you, surely there will be
a transformation. Remember, God told Abraham that if He would not
destroy Sodom and Gomorrah if Abraham could find only ten righteous
men. Unfortunately, he couldn't identify them. It is difficult to find
true people of God, but your prayer could make a significant difference.
Champion courses that will return all glory to God and draw people back
to God. It might be a challenge in an environment with religious tension,

but start and leave the rest to God. Daniel's dedication to God impacted a nation positively and all glory was returned to Almighty God.

Expose Abuse of Power and Injustice

> Ascribe to the LORD, O families of nations, ascribe to the LORD glory and strength. Ascribe to the LORD the glory due His name; bring an offering and come into His courts. (Psalm 96:7–8)

Many kings in the Bible did evil in the sight of God and either died or lost the throne. They engaged in all forms of idolatry, corruption, and rebellion. They are not far from the reality of today, which is why most nations are unproductive. Leadership lacks integrity, and anarchy has become the order of the day. People no longer consider the God factor in their decisions. As a child of God, you must find opportunities to highlight these examples to the leadership of your nation. These could be in the form of events or articles in the print media. The electronic media is full of content that promotes corruption and immorality. It's about time Christians rose up to take ownership of this access to share content that edifies a nation and gives glory to God. Use every opportunity to promote a life of holiness and righteousness. Stories in the Bible where the abuse of power led to untold suffering, hardship, and destruction to a nation should be represented as documentaries or movies. These projects should be backed by prayer and spiritual guidance to ensure it ultimately reaches the targeted audience. Give anointed men and women of God opportunities to proclaim the gospel of Jesus Christ and win souls to God. Righteousness exalts a nation, but sin is a reproach, and someone needs to teach and preach it repeatedly to impact the lives of people. It requires boldness and courage that comes only from God through Jesus Christ. He repeatedly told His anointed ones in multiple verses in the Bible to be of good courage. "Who is it that overcomes the world? Only he who believes that Jesus is the Son of God." (James 5:5).

Inspire the Next Generation of Leaders

> I have told you these things, so that in me you may have peace. In this world you will have trouble. But take heart! I have overcome the world. (John 16:33)

The future of every nation depends on the younger generation. Succession is inevitable, so the longer a nation fails to recognize the called and chosen amongst the next generation, the more unproductive it will remain. David was long anointed to be king even while Saul was still ruling. Samuel was identified as a priest even while Eli was still alive. Moses laid hands on Joshua as one who would lead the children of Israel to the Promised Land long before Moses died. Identifying with the next generation opens the door for mentorship, innovation, and creativity. It releases a new level of grace required to usher in a season that could end the infertility of a nation. Oftentimes, the older generation holds onto power until their dying day to the detriment of the people. It is an act of wickedness and covetousness. They amass wealth for their family who will squander everything within a few years after they die; wealth that could have provided better infrastructure and improved the standard of living of a nation. Leaders should think about legacy and not be shortsighted. What will you be remembered for by the next generation?

Give younger people access to leadership. Appoint them in positions of power and provide mentorship. Have a strategy for using the talents and skills God has endowed them with. Joseph, Joshua, and Daniel changed the destiny of their nations. Even in times of difficult economic crisis and famine, the nation of Egypt thrived under Joseph. In times of great wars and battles, Israel remained victorious under Joshua. Daniel found himself in really difficult environments, yet his excellent spirit separated him for a promotion into a position of influence.

Spirit of Compromise

> Now I am going to him who sent me, yet none of you asks me, "Where are you going?" (John 16:5)

A clear sign of a derailed nation is one where no one is asking the right questions. Everyone is busy trying to take a share of the national cake by all means and regardless of who gets hurt. This shows a lack of love and willingness to compromise on values to get ahead. Compromise sows seeds of bribery and corruption, ultimately consuming the appetite of the people and introducing unproductivity into the systems of government. Leadership during the reign of many kings and judges allowed this spirit of compromise to overwhelm them, which ultimately destroyed them and delayed the promise of the nation. Even leaders who start well get carried way by the debased nature of their environment and the depraved minds of sycophants and influential people around them. Instead of correcting the injustice done to the people, they celebrate these people in order to attract their loyalty and execute their agenda. As a chosen one of God, you should learn to ask the right questions using every opportunity available to you. However, it must be according to God's will for your life to ensure that you receive the grace for the opposition that might follow. Once you have been anointed for this national assignment according God's will, HE will defend HIS own.

Ministry

> Some have wandered away from these and turned to meaningless talk. (1 Timothy 1:6)

A call to ministry is a divine assignment ordained by God Himself. He has entrusted you with His Word to deliver to His people. The emphasis here is on "His." It belongs to Him, not to you. Therefore, if you carry out ministry the way you believe God has told you, and He also says that He will build His church and that the gate of hell shall not prevail, why are you experiencing infertility in ministry?

Idolatry Causes the Water to Dry Up

> A drought on her waters! They will dry up. For it is a land of idols, idols that will go mad with terror. (Jeremiah 50:38)

It is very easy to derail from a call of ministry to idolatry. As a minister of God and hopefully an astute student of the Bible, idolatry should have no place in your private and public life. Your ministry activities should neither seek nor tolerate any form of sin and idolatry introduced either to the leadership or membership of the church. Do an in-depth study of the concept idolatry in the Bible and examine yourself. What door have you opened into your ministry? What really happens in the secret chambers of your life and ministry? What do you permit and approve amongst your stewards? These answers are not only capable of causing the drought but will also go from extreme chaos to utter destruction if you do not repent and return to God. If it is true that God has called you, you must return to God in prayer and ask for mercy. The golden calf built by Aaron for the children of Israel could not exist in the same atmosphere as the tablet containing the Ten Commandments of God received by Moses. The prophets of Baal could not call down fire, but Elijah did in the same environment. If you can no longer demonstrate the power of God in your ministry, you have to seek the face of God urgently before destruction befalls you and your followers. Where you still do not understand the nature of what has befallen you, seek counsel from another servant of God.

Family Ties

> Then a teacher of the law came to him and said, "Teacher, I will follow you wherever you go." Jesus replied, "Foxes have holes and birds of the air have nests, but the Son of Man has no place to lay his head." Another disciple said to him, "Lord, first let me go and bury my father." But Jesus told him, "Follow me, and let the dead bury their own dead." (Matthew 8:19–22)

Jesus Christ paid a price for us. Your divine assignment calls for a level of love and service that will definitely impact your immediate family and friends. To serve God effectively and prevent infertility in your ministry, you have to make sacrifices. At the altar of prayer, continue to ask for grace to manage the impact on your parents, spouse, and kids, for only God can take care of His own, and He can much better than you. When the Lord permits, spend quality time with them and ensure that they are well grounded in the knowledge of God. Get them actively involved in church activities because that builds the foundation for their divine assignment. By their association with a servant of God, they have been ordained into divine destiny too. You ought to provide nourishment until they identify spiritual parents and mentors. Instability in your family will ultimately affect you and your ministry; therefore, ensure you do not neglect your family. In everything you do, do not forsake your calling and ministry by clinging to family. Ask God for the grace to create that balance in love, respect, and faithfulness. In some cases, family will constitute the obstacle to ministry. Spouses will be the opposition to your calling and children will create the distraction through unwholesome behavior that impacts your credibility as a servant of God. In all this, we are more than conquerors. Eli lost his ministry because of his family, but Jacob's family formed the nation of Israel and earned him a gift of infertility. Continuously seek God's face and remain in spirit to discern the reason for the season. It could be a new phase emerging for your ministry and family. Therefore, your countenance and response must not be controlled by the external factors around you. Focus on your divine calling, and always remember the first time God made you aware of a ministry for Him. God will never leave you or forsake you, but you have to be found faithful in your divine assignment to receive the gift of infertility.

Ministry Is a Higher Calling

> Jesus said to them, "I tell you the truth, at the renewal of all things, when the Son of Man sits on his glorious throne, you who have followed me will also sit on twelve thrones, judging the twelve tribes of Israel." (Matthew 19:28)

It is high calling; therefore, challenges and circumstances around you will be subject to attacks and battles. If you are faithful and in right standing with God, a cycle of unexplained, difficult events, causing seasons of drought, could be a sign of expansion. You should take advantage of these circumstances by seeking God like never before. Every new level in ministry will attract reciprocal battles, but you have been equipped to weather the storm and conquer. It's not a time to deceive or exploit your members but a reason to activate spiritual exercises and fellowship like never before. Invite true servants of God to minister in and nourish your church; however, beware of false teachers and prophets (2 Peter 2). Raise the level of worship and spend time in your secret place of prayer. Every man of God in the Bible knew when to retreat to prepare for a new level ministry. Furthermore, the fruits of the Holy Spirit should abound in your life and ministry. Leave no room for the infiltration of evil ones (1 Peter 4–5). Establish clearly articulated programs for the church, especially the induction and indoctrination of new members and workers. Be careful about people in leadership and those who seem to have significant influence on the mood and activities of your ministry. Do not tolerate anyone who sows discord in the church, no matter how significant they are in the church. Ignorance cannot be an excuse for your divine assignment. Giving should follow principles clearly stated in the Bible. Lastly, you have been called to proclaim the true and authentic Word of God; therefore, you must live, preach, and teach the truth, no matter how difficult. You cannot grow in ministry if you are afraid of losing your members by speaking the truth. If you are being careful or seeking to be politically correct in the pulpit, you will continue to experience infertility in ministry. Sin is sin, no matter who is committing unholy and unrighteous acts, especially in the church. What you have chosen to be silent about will ultimately destroy what you seek to protect. Be guided by the Holy Spirit and not counsel from yourself or mortal men.

Be careful about the integrity and credibility of men and women of God you associate with, for Jude 1:12 says,

> These men are blemishes at your love feasts, eating with you without the slightest qualm—shepherds who feed only themselves. They are clouds without rain, blown along by the wind, autumn trees, without fruit and uprooted—twice dead.

Don't mortgage your ministry on the altar of popularity and worldly influence. Trust God to build your church and make appropriate divine connections relevant to your ministry and the people, His sheep, that only

He will send to your ministry. Therefore, teach them only the Word of God and wisdom that is inspired by the Holy Spirit. The Bible is your reference point. Revelation 22:18–19 says,

> I warn everyone who hears the words of prophecy of this book: If anyone adds anything to them, God will add to him the plagues described in this book. And if anyone takes words away from this book of prophecy, God will take away from him his share in the tree of life and in the holy city, which are described in this book.

CHAPTER 15

Glimpse of the Glory of God

That I may publish with the voice of thanksgiving, and tell of all thy wondrous works. (Psalm 26:7 KJV)

In John 11:33, Jesus Christ was deeply moved in spirit and troubled when he saw Mary, Lazarus's sister, weeping. Jesus wept too in verse 35. This goes to show that the Lord is deeply moved by our pain. But He also used that opportunity to preach. He reminds us in verse forty that all we need is to believe and we will see the glory of God. If the reason for your infertility is for God's glory, it must be for your good. Jesus Christ had no doubt whatsoever that Lazarus would be raised from the death, so He went ahead to make the most profound prayer any believer should say once he or she is at the edge of his or her breakthrough: a prayer of thanksgiving. Your testimony is here, and your deliverance has arrived. The stone has been rolled away.

An Atmosphere of Thanksgiving

> So they took away the stone. Then Jesus looked up and said, "Father, I thank you that you have heard me. I knew that you always hear me, but I said this for the benefit of the people standing here, that they may believe that you sent me." (John 11:41–42)

You have been through everything, and now your resurrection is here.

God has constantly assured you in the midst of all your troubles that He would never leave you or forsake you. Perhaps it has taken longer than necessary or longer than you expected. The greatest testimony is resilience and living to testify what the Lord has done. Your gift of infertility will only manifest in an atmosphere of thanksgiving. You must remain steadfast in faith to finish this race successfully. You have been through severe suffering, but it's no longer time to weep, doubt, and complain. This is not the time to worry about your enemies because God has taken over the battle. Simply guard over your conviction that God is about to come through for you. Just know in your heart that your time has come. It is time to thank God and await the delivery of your special gift.

It's Personal!

> Meditate upon these things; give thyself wholly to them; that thy profiting may appear to all. (1 Timothy 4:15 KJV)

In every race and marathon, it doesn't matter how many people you trained or practiced with before that day; the running and final victory belongs to you. It is all about your performance on that day, all by yourself. It is about what you have invested in prayer, practice, and perseverance. Your coach and pastors can cheer you on, but if you fall on the tracks, you have lost the race. A woman in labor goes through the birth process all by herself, despite the number of doctors and family friends awaiting the news of the baby. She has to remember everything she was taught and obey critical final instructions from doctors and midwives. However, doctors and midwives are also guided by the sights and sounds of motherhood. Motherhood at that moment is about the woman and the baby. Similarly, as you approach the finishing line, you have to create personal time to commune with God. Reduce the noise around you so you can discern the approach of your testimony. It doesn't matter how much false evidence you see, hold onto that clear word from God that tells you your gift of infertility is here. Noah knew that storm was over, so he sent the first bird and then the second bird to verify. The blind man could not see very well the first time, but as long as he had entered that the atmosphere of healing, a second touch from Jesus Christ opened his eyes. Isaiah stayed in the same position expecting the much-awaited rain until his servant saw just a tiny cloud. The glory of God is not cheap. You have to exercise discipline and complete trust in the faithfulness of God.

Golden Couples Waiting for the Fruit of the Womb

You will arise and have compassion on Zion, for it is time
to show favor to her; the appointed time has come. (Psalm
102:13)

How long have you waited for the fruit of the womb? Have you been
listening for a divine direction required to move your destiny forward?
Do you realize that you were created and sent to impact a generation?
Do you realize that the fruit you are seeking is not ordinary and you may
need to be processed to accept and nurture this divine gift from God?

Your gift of infertility is beyond your tears. It is a blessing to the world.
The blessing you desire right now might be completely separate from your
assignment. Your heart's desire may or may not be your ministry, but it
keeps you focused, engaged, and hopefully available to be used by God.
If you are currently seeking the fruit of the womb, God said, "None shall
be barren," (Exodus 23:26) so that settles it. Your difference is in that
difficulty. Your victory resides in the victim you think you are. Your heart's
desire may be your access to God's plan for your life.

Struggling with infertility of the womb for many years is one of
the most grueling yet rewarding experiences in life. You are forced to
reexamine yourself and challenge everything you have ever done and
believed but set your priorities and purpose in place. The gift of infertility

is beyond just creating a family. Although the process is tough, the fruit is divine. It has to be for the glory of God!

Sustaining a Positive Countenance

Eli answered, "Go in peace, and may the God of Israel grant you what you have asked of him." She said, "May your servant find favor in your eyes." Then she went her way and ate something, and her face was no longer downcast. (1 Samuel 1:17–18)

It is not always easy. Some days will be better than others. But you should learn to live above your circumstances. Remain calm and believe God. Be still and know that He is God. His word is yea and amen. God loves you!

You will find the earlier section on coping with infertility of the womb useful. Also, the following should help you maintain a positive countenance during the waiting period:

- **Cherish the process**. The pain is part of the journey, and you will live to remember it with joy and no more tears. Your mess will become your message, testimony, and access to your gift. Repetition of some activities and boredom can trigger depressive moods and make your trial period more difficult to cope with. Learn to explore new interests, and challenge yourself to discover new activities. In Genesis, Sarah faithfully followed Abraham from one location to another, often supporting his motives, exploring new activities, and enjoying their wealth.
- **Nurture your family relationships**. These may or may not be your biological family. They could be immediate or external, such as church members. They will always be there for you through your trials and uphold you in prayer, especially when you become spiritually weak.
- **Sieve your friendships and all relationships in general**. Do not be under pressure to sustain relationships that trigger negative feelings or make you say or do things against your faith and

convictions. Be decisive about cutting off such companions, as their negative influence could rob you of the progress you have made so far. Rachel's envy of and competitiveness with her sister made her seek alternative solutions to her problem by offering her maidservants to her husband and strife with her sister until she refocused on God and gave birth to Joseph (Genesis 30:22–24), a child of promise and a mighty servant of God.

- **Focus on the package and compartmentalize issues**. Accept daily experiences as part of the process, and when unrelated issues come up, treat them separately and ensure not to carry over these matters. Don't be overly sensitive to issues. You have enough challenges. Do not add any more to them. Guard your five senses seriously, as these are access points to the most depressing and irritating issues. Esther was convinced to participate in a beauty pageant. She won, but little did she know that her real battles would save a whole nation.

- **Speak to your future.** Do not let your problem define you and determine your future. It is very common to postpone and reschedule plans in order to make room for expected blessings. Do not put your future on hold. Your birthing process might be hidden in something in your future. Ruth was determined to follow her mother-in-law to a new location, and there she found her destiny (Ruth 1:16).

- **Explore your instincts. Don't close yourself to options**. In your high moments, when you are in an excellent spiritual disposition, take note of all new ideas. Write them down and begin to work on them. These issues may access the solution you seek. Writing them down helps you remember, as it is very easy to dismiss positive thoughts when in depressive moods. Reading these notes at such times will also give you something to look forward to. Ruth learned to glean with the reapers, a task she had never done before, and in the process caught the attention of her destiny helper, Boaz (Ruth 2:7).

- **Smile through the tears**. When you become so overwhelmed and feel like crying, remember that you are more than a conqueror and in the end you will testify. It's okay to let the tears flow, but don't lose your focus on God. He is the author and finisher of your faith, and He is well able to give you your heart's desire according to His will. Smile! Jesus Christ loves you!

- **Create a memorial**. In your trial, celebrate milestones, successes, and victories. Thank God for all mercies and worship Him. In the Bible, Abraham and his descendants always built an altar everywhere they went, especially when they encountered God's mercy and favor. Each altar represented something to the glory of God. Throughout this journey, Abraham and Sarah were barren, but they listened to and obeyed every command from God. No wonder God called Abraham His friend. James 1:22–27 and Luke 6:46–49 also expound on the importance of listening to and doing what the Word of God says, creating everlasting memorials.

- **Grieve sweetly**. Your infertility may have been caused by grief over a lost loved one, like Naomi and her daughters-in-law (Ruth 1:11–13) or a miscarriage, death of a child, or stillbirth. It is not the end. It's painful, but remember, God is in complete control! He alone has the final say. The chosen one will live. If it's a health issue, you'll be healed; if it's a generational issue, your deliverance is around the corner. You have a destiny and a divine assignment to fulfill and execute, so focus on God and seek Him earnestly. As soon as David realized that the child Uriah's wife, Bathsheba, bore him had died, he stopped grieving and moved on. God then blessed him with a son, Solomon, whom God endowed with wisdom and riches. Solomon later became king and built the tabernacle for God.

- **Share your thoughts**. Sometimes sharing a burden with your spouse, trusted friend, or a spiritual counselor, such as your pastor, can help you cope. Ultimately, God's Word should be your reference point. Meditate on it day and night, and believe what God says about your situation. No one can pray your prayer for you. Hannah shared her thoughts and misery with the priest (or pastor) in 1 Samuel 1:15–16 and received comfort. God blessed her soon after that encounter. The interaction with Eli the priest focused her attention on God instead of her condition, which ultimately changed her countenance.

- **Seek a place of worship**. As emphasized in earlier chapters, your spiritual state gives you access to your ultimate gift of infertility. This is mostly nurtured within an environment that is filled with the Spirit of God and a Bible-believing church. Hannah always went to Shiloh, the religious center of the nation, and God answered her prayers there at His own appointed time (1 Samuel 1:9–11). No doubt her prayers at this very location provoked God to remember her. While you can create a worship place at home, also attend church and participate in activities that nurture your destiny and glorify God. But be sure to keep your eyes focused on Jesus to avoid anxiety and exhaustion (Luke 11:41–42).
- **Forgive yourself**. God can use anybody. It doesn't matter how bad your sin may have been. If there's anything in your past that still hurts or haunts you, confess it, forgive yourself, and move on. Old things have passed away and all things have become new. Holding onto unforgiveness of any kind is poisonous to your body, soul, and spirit. Also, release the people who hurt you so God can hear your prayers (Luke 11:4). Rahab was a prostitute, Moses was a murderer, and David committed adultery and killed the woman's husband to cover his sin. Mary Magdalene was caught in adultery and also had seven demons. Peter denied Jesus three times. All these are true, but look at the critical roles these people played in the Bible and then achieved their gifts of infertility of character. Rahab was in the lineage of Jesus Christ, Moses delivered God's chosen people (Israel), and Mary Magdalene played a critical role in the divine ministry of our Lord, Jesus Christ.
- **Celebrate with others and share their joy**. During your waiting time, life goes on. Other people will receive the very gifts and blessings you have desired for so long. You must celebrate with others. God is looking to see your countenance. We all have our different destinies; nothing about the moment is a final conclusion about your life. You must trust God's timing and purposes for your life. Elizabeth celebrated her cousin Mary and sang for her (Luke 1:39–45), and Mary returned all the praise to God in "The Magnificat" (Luke 1:46–55). This should be the reaction and response of all Christians to the blessings of God. It's not how

long you've waited for the blessing but how your gift of infertility returns glory to God.

- **Count your blessings**. Similarly, while you are waiting, other aspects of your life may be flourishing. Living in good health alone and being alive is a blessing. Talking, seeing, and eating are all luxuries that some people don't have. Celebrate your victories and successes. God will complete what He has started. The Samarian woman who Jesus met at the well simply ran off to preach the gospel after she had an encounter with Jesus.

Remember, God's purpose is larger than your pain!

Father, the time has come. Glorify your Son, that your Son may glorify you. For you granted him authority over all people that he might give eternal life to all those you have given him. Now this is eternal life: that they may know you, the only true God, and Jesus Christ, whom you have sent. I have brought you glory on earth by completing the work you gave me to do. And now, Father, glorify me in your presence with the glory I had with you before the world began. (John 17:1–5)

ABOUT THE AUTHOR

Nothing in life prepared me for a long and dynamic journey to fertility. On the trip were high and lows, victories and failures, celebration and grief, a stern revelation of what life could hold for one unprepared for the consequences of signing up to be in the will of GOD. Building a career and making choices but realizing in the end that the only road to resolving the dilemma was to accept the commission that CHRIST had revealed to me in Matthew 6:33. That revelation changed my life completely, challenged every assumption or belief I always had in life and gave me room to embrace my gift. My deep desire to share the victory of that journey overwhelms me to the point where I often times have a sense of emptiness yet the confidence to know that HE who has started a good work in me shall complete it to HIS glory and honour.

Nnenna has expertise in financial services including many years experience from three international banks. She is also a Sloan Fellow with degrees in Finance, Leadership and Strategy. Despite her outstanding education and career, Nnenna has a deep desire to constantly search for the mind of GOD and seek the will of GOD. She has held leadership positions in ministry but this book is born out of her personal experience. It will speak to your heart and encourage you to know that you are not alone with GOD as you go in search of your divine destiny.

Printed in the United States
By Bookmasters